INTRODUCTION TO HAND Lettering

MYE DE LEON

What is Hand-Lettering?

Hand-lettering is the art of drawing letters by hand. We use words to communicate but the way we hand-letter those words can also convey a subtle message. This book introduces you to a wide variety of different styles of lettering and shows you how to use them to create awesome designs that will amaze your family and friends!

Using this Book

This informative opening section will introduce you to the hand-lettering essentials, providing you with the foundation skills you'll need to master the following six sections of the book. Each of these sections are themed with different hand-lettering styles, ranging from more traditional Blackletter-style lettering to comic- and cartoon-style lettering. It's amazing how you can evoke a particular mood, a vibrant theme, or even a specific historical period just by carefully choosing the lettering style you use! The final section allows you to apply your new hand-lettering knowledge to general composition skills and includes an exciting range of projects to help you become a true hand-lettering maestro!

This book includes over seventy-five alphabets, activities, and projects to complete! The projects range from creating a personalized birthday card for someone special to designing a calligraphic-style motivational poster that you can frame and hang on your wall, and even to digitizing your lettering and using it to personalize a photo! Beware though: this book may result in family and friends begging you to write signs for them, pleading with you to compose pretty invitations, and insisting on regular handwritten letters!

Let's start by learning a little more about hand-lettering. First off, let's establish the difference between hand-lettering, calligraphy, and typography, as people often confuse these.

Hand-Lettering

Typically, hand-lettering is completely free-form, unique, and usually created for a single use only, although in practice you can trace your favorite designs while you're learning or trying out new methods. Above all, hand-lettering is about drawing and having fun; it has guidelines but few rules.

Calligraphy

Calligraphy is handwritten rather than hand-drawn script. It joins letters together into words using a broad-tipped instrument like a dip pen or brush and largely follows established alphabets and rules. Calligraphy is also evenly balanced writing, often in old-fashioned but beautiful Copperplate script. It is a discipline through which you learn controlled penmanship and compositional form, so is less free-form than hand-lettering.

Typography

Typography is the design of printed letters. While it is also about making visually appealing letters, typography is different from hand-lettering in that the exact style of letter can be replicated again and again. It involves selecting typefaces (fonts), choosing sizes (point sizes), and adjusting the spaces above and below letters (leading) and between letters (kerning) and words (tracking). Typographers combine and arrange existing commercial typefaces and fonts to enhance their overall design. You can still learn a lot from calligraphy and typography to apply to your hand-lettering!

So now that you know a little about hand-lettering, let's get started and learn how to create it ourselves!

Lettering TOOLS

You don't need specialist tools to begin lettering: inexpensive art supplies bought at your local store are a great place to start. The tools shown below are really useful. As you progress, you may want to explore some of the more specialized equipment, like those shown on the facing page.

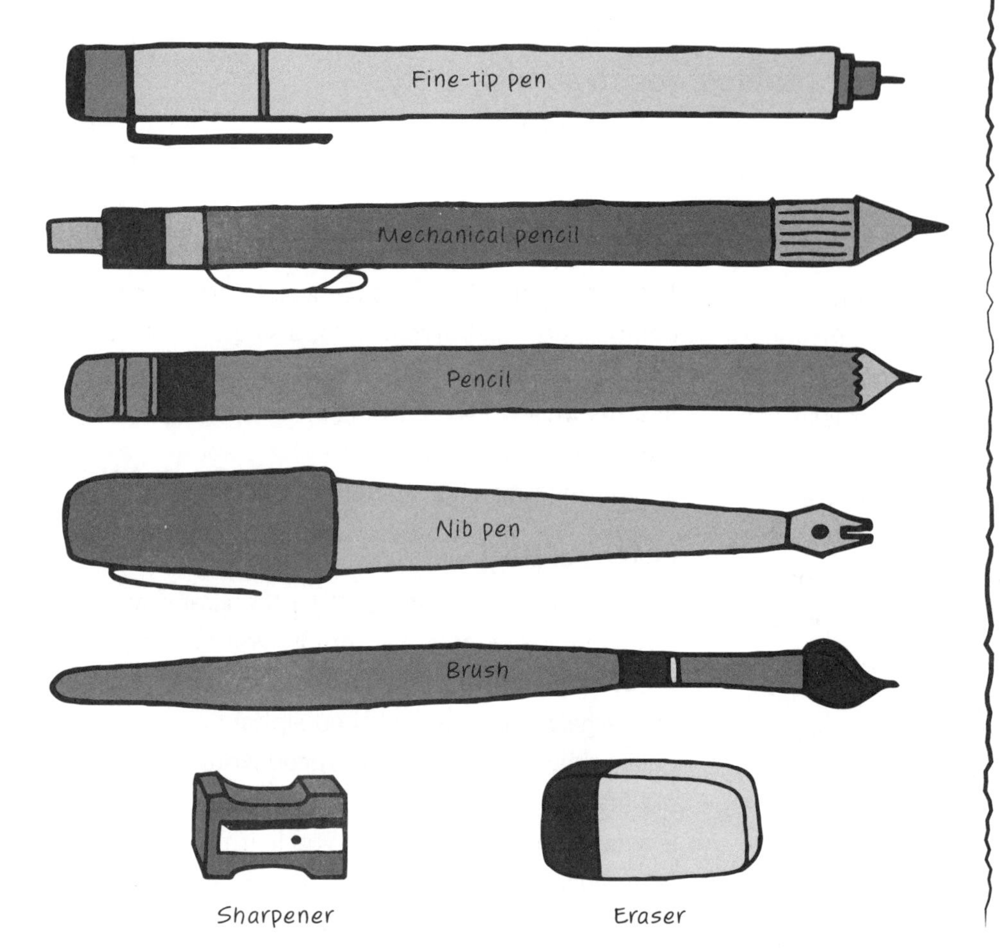

Fine-tip pen: modern writing tool that allows precise lettering. The tip can vary between being wide and very fine. The ink is stored within the pen.

Mechanical pencil: generally consists of a plastic handle and a mechanically propelled thin lead core. They are primarily used for technical drawing and precise lettering.

Pencil: most have a graphite core, usually varying between 9H (the hardest) to 9B (the softest), with F and HB being within the medium range. With these you can produce a wide variety of tones from light gray (the hardest pencil) to black (the softest pencil).

Nib pen or dip pen: consists of a handle with a removable metal nib at the end that is dipped into ink every few letters. There is no ink stored within the pen.

Brush: traditionally used for some forms of lettering. This historically consists of a bamboo handle and a tip made from animal hair. Cheaper brushes are made from synthetics.

Ruler: important for straight lines, especially in the planning stage of hand-lettering.

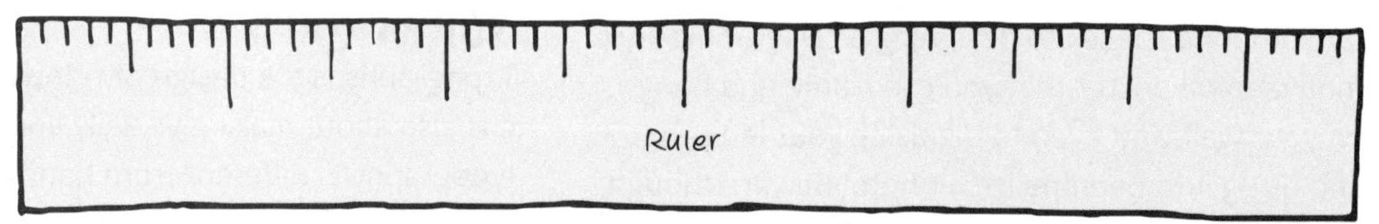

Paper: good quality drawing paper is best because it allows repeated use of the eraser. Alternatively, you can use tracing paper to copy the finalized design on to a fresh piece of paper.

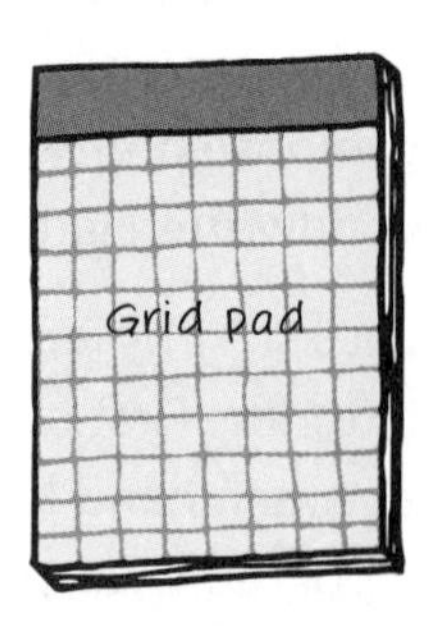

Dot and grid pads: particularly useful for beginners as guidelines to help create even lettering.

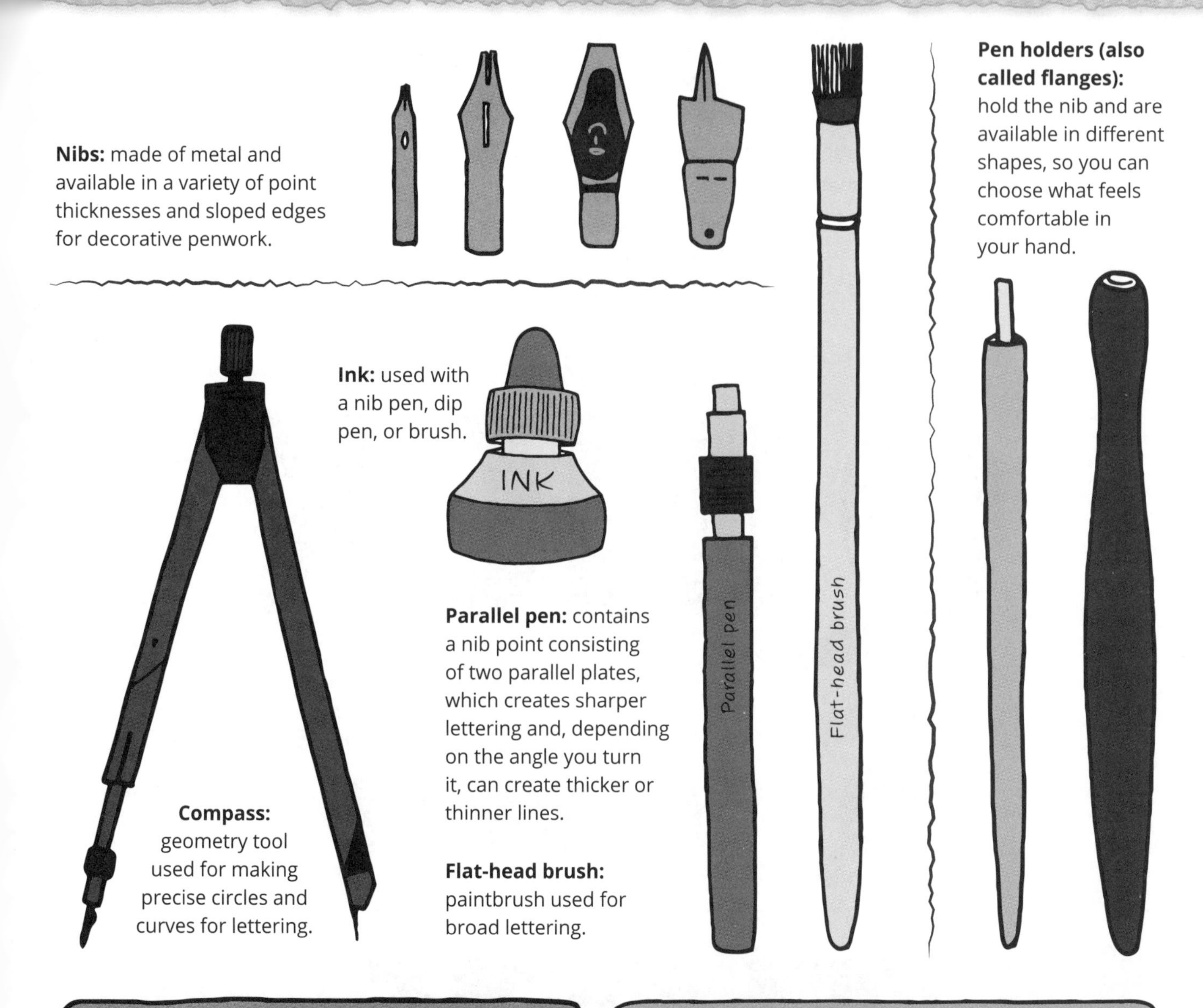

Nibs: made of metal and available in a variety of point thicknesses and sloped edges for decorative penwork.

Pen holders (also called flanges): hold the nib and are available in different shapes, so you can choose what feels comfortable in your hand.

Ink: used with a nib pen, dip pen, or brush.

Compass: geometry tool used for making precise circles and curves for lettering.

Parallel pen: contains a nib point consisting of two parallel plates, which creates sharper lettering and, depending on the angle you turn it, can create thicker or thinner lines.

Flat-head brush: paintbrush used for broad lettering.

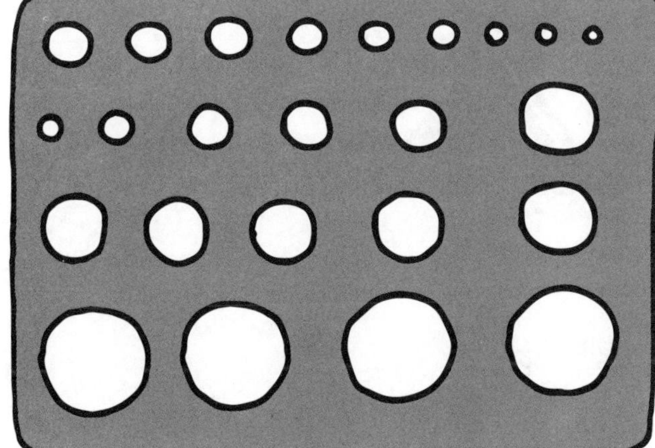

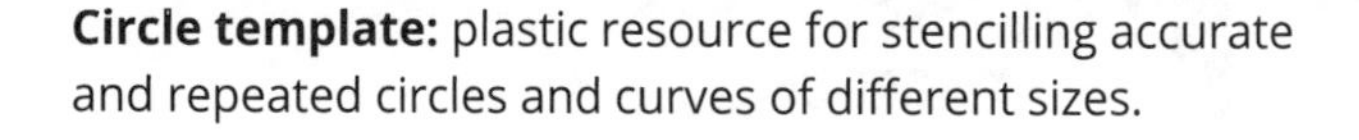

Circle template: plastic resource for stencilling accurate and repeated circles and curves of different sizes.

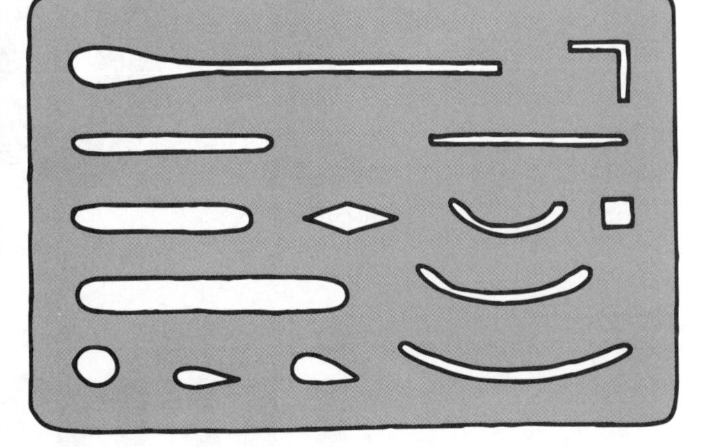

Erasing shield: a thin sheet of steel or plastic with slots and holes that allow an eraser to be used through them. They are useful to protect work from messy blots and smudges, or from accidentally erasing other parts of the composition.

Lettering TERMINOLOGY

Understanding lettering terms gives you a good sense of how each part of a letter is formed and how you can use that knowledge to create variety. The basic principle for lettering is that it should look good but also that you should be able to read it easily. That's why it is important to understand how each stroke works—you want everyone to be able to read and enjoy what you have written!

The sentence across these two pages contains every letter of the alphabet with annotations of common and important lettering terms. When you are familiar with the terms and the parts of the letters, you'll have a better grasp of how to play with them so you can create more unique pieces of artwork. Make these lettering terms your buddies and call them by their names!

Lettering TERMINOLOGY

Think of a letter as being like a person. You can begin by drawing the letter frame (also called a skeleton), then add weight and definition (which is like adding muscles and skin), then style (like clothing), and finally add any embellishments (like hats, shoes, and jewelry)!

skeleton PRACTICE

weight PRACTICE

style PRACTICE

embellishments PRACTICE

Use tracing paper to discover the many ways you can shape and style a single letter. Start by drawing the main body of the letter A on white paper. Then, using tracing paper, trace it again and again, over and over, varying a small detail each time. Below are some examples to get you started. Enjoy experimenting!

skeleton weight embellishment

A A A

A A A

A A A

A A A

Let's look at the three fundamental styles of hand-lettering: serif, sans-serif, and script. This is a great starting point that will allow you to develop different lettering styles, as well as to explore which type suits which situation or project.

A serif is a small line attached at the top or bottom (or both) of the main strokes of a letter. It was developed by carvers in ancient Roman times when letters were hammered into stone. A serif made the individual letters easier to distinguish from each other. Early printers used serif fonts for books and newspapers as it was believed that they made reading easier. Serifs can also be used to make lettering look more serious and important.

Slab serif

CAMP

Slab serif

Sans-serif

Decorative serif

TIP

The "CHEERS" lettering is already decorative, so it doesn't necessarily need any extra surrounding embellishments to look ornate.

EVERY MOMENT

MATTERS

Bracketed serif

Bracketed serif

HAPPY

EVER AFTER

Bracketed & hairline serif

Hairline serif

SERIF

The various serif endings give a different feel to your lettering: the slab serif is a no-nonsense look that is good for things like important notices, while the gothic serif is rather more whimsical and attention-grabbing, so it's good for party invitations and posters.

Gothic serif

Cupped serif

SLEEP

Slab bracketed serif

Gothic, cupped, and slab bracketed serif

Tuscan serif

SUPER

Tuscan, bracketed, & slab serifs all working together for a super serif piece!

The key to serif success is to make sure that they are consistent and similar across all letters within a word. As a general rule, serifs shouldn't extend far from the main letter strokes, although, of course, it's up to you how you want your lettering to look!

A

Regular serif

A

Condensed serif

A

Extended serif

SANS-SERIF

Sans-serif is a style of lettering without any accents or strokes attached to the main letter strokes. The word *sans* is a French word that means "without." Sans-serif script first appeared in the 5th century BC but disappeared during the Classical revival in the Renaissance (in the 15th and 16th centuries), reappearing in the 20th century with a more streamlined, modern look. Because they are easier to read, sans-serif fonts are often used for children's books. It is a relaxed style for hand-lettering, ideal for more informal projects and messages.

Plain sans-serif lettering can add real impact to your message and can be great for making bold statements like these examples.

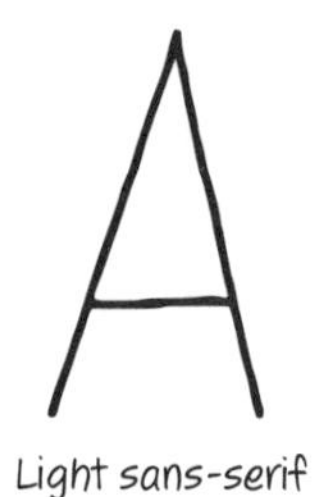

Light sans-serif

Regular sans-serif

Bold sans-serif

One way to be playful with your sans-serifs is to add effects! Use a rectangular shape as a guide for your hand-lettering to add depth to your letters. You can even draw simple block shapes coming out from the letter stems to create a 3-D effect. Careful use of shading can make the 3-D effect even more dramatic by highlighting each letter differently, making it look as though they're jumping out off the page!

LOVE
YOURSELF

SANS-SERIF

So, for a modern feel, why not try sans-serif lettering? It has no frills. It's clean and has a strong visual impact, and gives your message a punch! For example, it's perfect for a whimsical soda-shop sign.

1. Write the letter skeletons faintly so you have a base to work around.

2. Fill out the letters so they have some "body."

3. Ink your design, adding in some cool effects like the ones below, and then erase the pencil marks. Outline the border around the text. For extra emphasis and a touch of fun, draw a soda bottle and add highlights and bubbles!

Add parallel mirror-style lines, giving a vintage feel.

Emphasize the letters by adding shading and lines around the outside, then add dots resembling bubbles on the inside.

Half-color in the letters as if they are half-filled with soda.

Script

Script is a handwriting-like style based on fluidly joining letters together using a nib or brush pen. The look is definitely eye-catching, but you must work it out carefully first or it can become messy and lose its effectiveness. When it's well done, like these elegant examples, it is a beautiful type of hand-lettering.

Perfect is Boring

Apple PIE

Laugh

Keep it Real

Catch your BREATH, Take your TIME

Alive

Congrats
GET Lucky
Awesome
Have No Fear
She Believed She Could so She Did
Quoted

Trace over the faint lettering below to help you practice writing in the script style of hand-lettering.

Stop Existing & Start Living

Now use this page to try copying the script lettering from the previous page from scratch or make up your own phrase to design in script style, inspired by what you have learned so far.

Don't worry if it's not perfect:
that individual touch is part of what makes hand-lettering so great!

Lettering DOs & DON'Ts

You need to understand the rules of hand-lettering before you can break them. Here are some guidelines you should follow to stop your letters from looking distorted or unbalanced. It's useful to have a look at some of the common errors first-time letterers make and learn how to avoid them.

Swirls

Like flounces on a fancy dress, swirls are great additions to make your piece prettier and more elegant. Just don't go swirl-crazy! Overdoing it can ruin your artwork: less can often be more.

Incorrect

This example has way too many flourishes. It looks unbalanced, messy, and hard to read.

Correct

This is much better: the swirls are stylish but not overdone. Simple yet elegant!

Strokes

When lettering M, N, and W, keep in mind that every second stroke should be made thicker, as shown below. It may seem awkward at first, but this rule is designed to ensure you can clearly read what these letters are; it also looks more attractive.

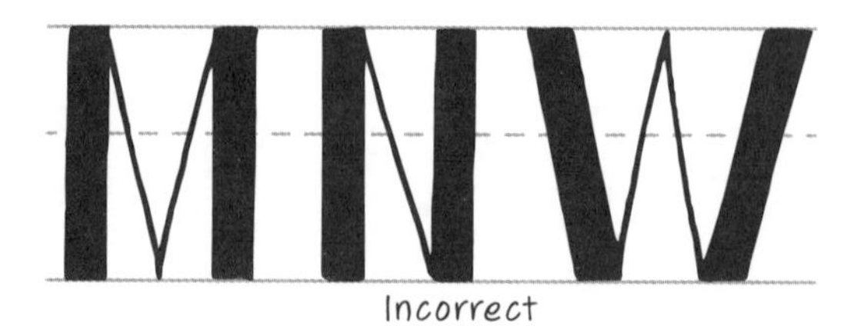

Incorrect

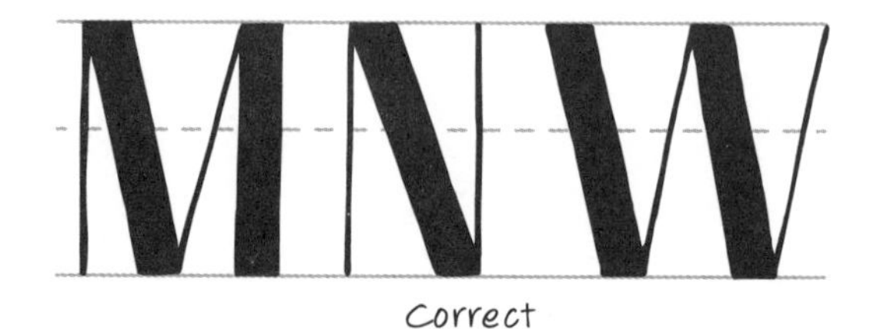

Correct

Curved and Pointed Letters

Curved letters (such as C, G, J, O, Q, U) and pointed letters (those with pointed apexes such as A, M, N, V, W) tend to extend above the height of the ascender line and below the baseline. This actually helps to create the illusion that they are the same height as the flat letters and helps with readability.

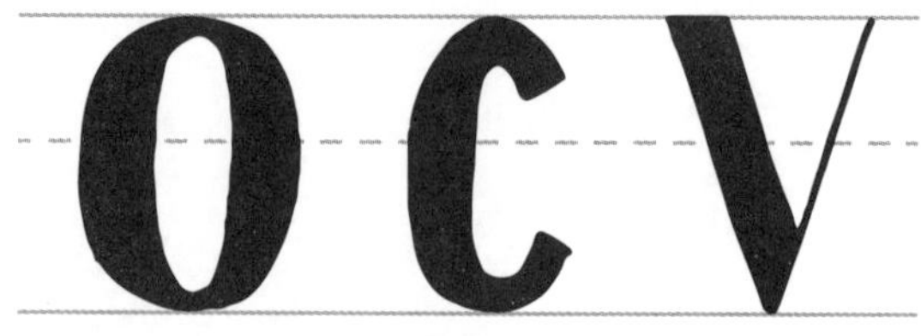

Incorrect

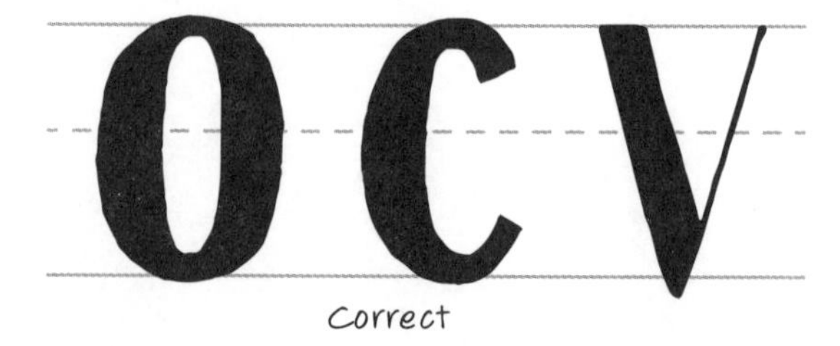

Correct

Flat Apexes

Pointed letters with flat apexes (like N, V, and sometimes A) must be treated differently. While they are technically classified as "pointed letters," you can hand-letter them in such a way that their apexes are flat. When you do this, the apexes should sit exactly along the ascender line and the baseline.

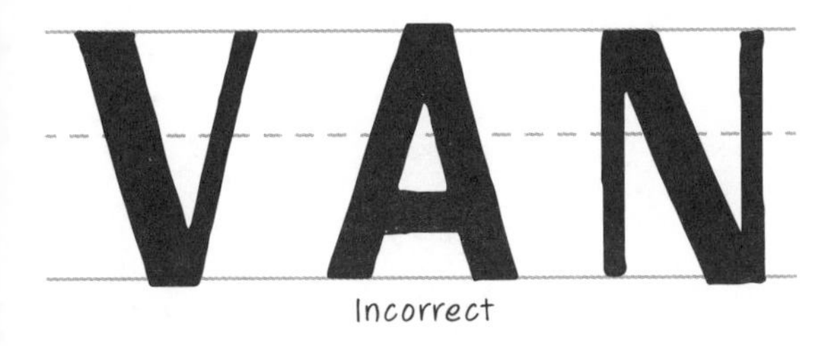

Incorrect

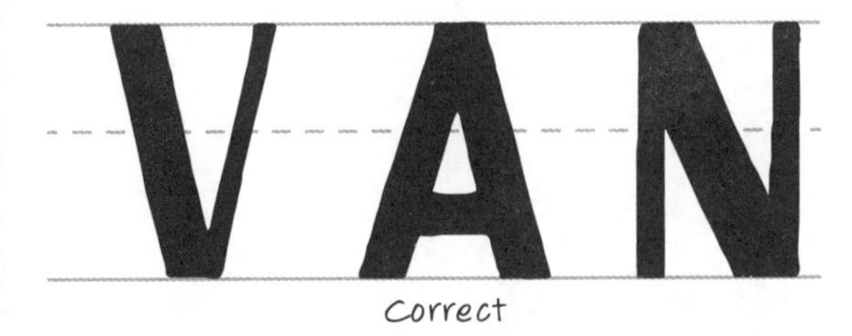

Correct

Crossbars

The crossbars of the letters E and F are sometimes tricky to make look proportional. Remember that the middle crossbar of an E and the lower crossbar of an F must be shorter (it makes it neater and more legible as well). And while they appear similar, the lower bar on the F is conventionally positioned slightly below the midline, which is lower than the bar of the E.

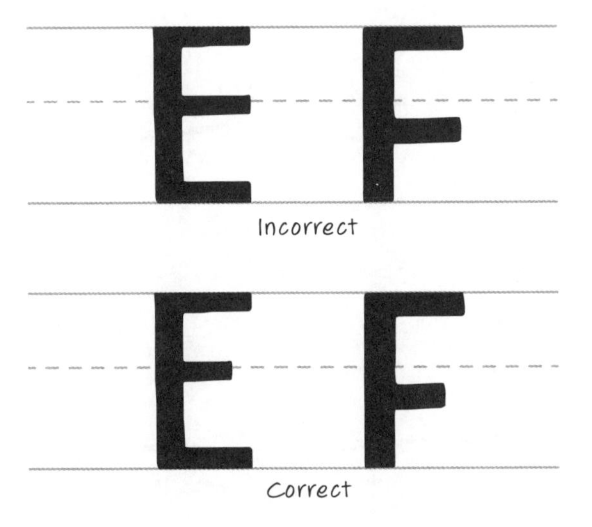

Proportions

Letters vary in their width-to-height proportions (their "measure"). Not only can the widths of letters in the same alphabet vary enormously, but different styles of alphabet vary in the space that they occupy, with some being tall and narrow, and others being short and wide. You can often instinctively tell when your letters are in the wrong proportion and as you become more experienced you will be able to recognize where you need to adjust their proportions until the lettering looks right. If it looks wrong, then it is wrong—so train your critical eye!

In this example, the P's stem is too high and its counter too narrow, the K's apex starts too high, and the W's apex is too low.

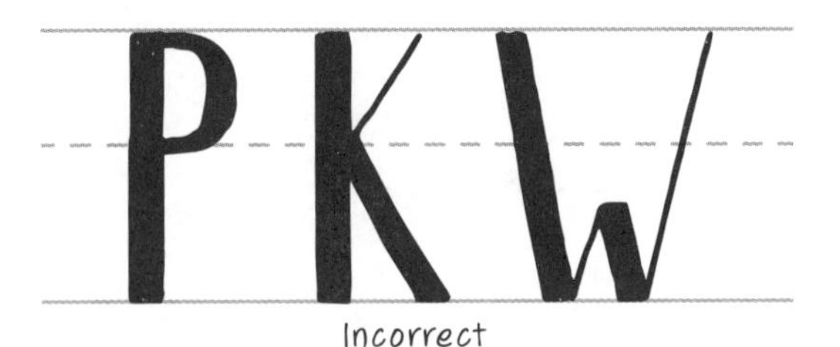

Incorrect

You can immediately see that these letters are in better proportion than in the first example, just from making the P's stem shorter and its counter wider, the K's apex lower, and the W's apex higher.

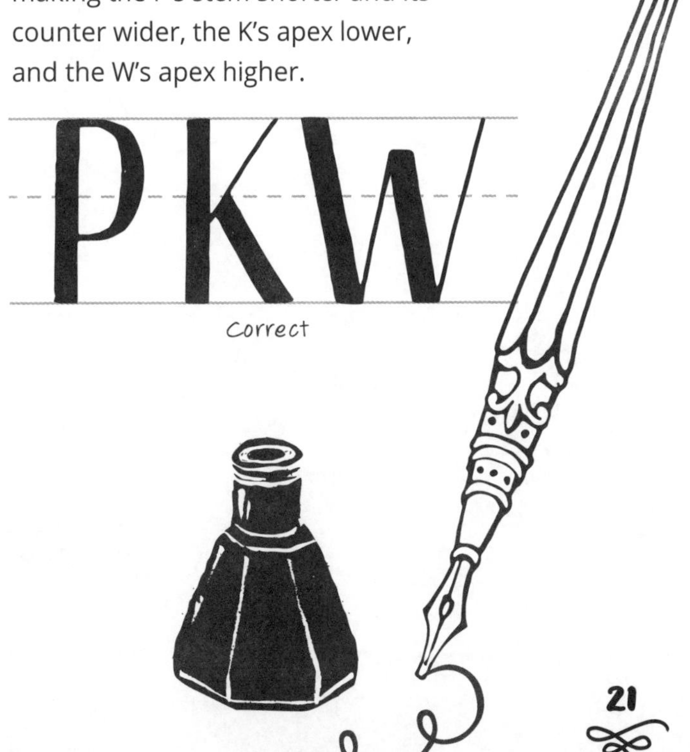

Correct

Flourishes, Borders, & EMBELLISHMENTS

Extravagant embellishments can be added to your lettering to make them look more fancy. Embellishments can be used to frame the words and are useful for hand-lettered cards and invitations. Here are a few examples to inspire you. Try adding some letters within these frames and banners to get an idea of their effect. Or you can practice the frame and banners within the frames themselves!

GOOD
NIGHT

Thank You!

Project Inspiration

The great thing about lettering is that once you have an understanding of the basic techniques, you can mix and match them to create your own style like the piece below does. Experiment and let your imagination run wild to see where it takes you!

REMEMBER,

PRACTICE

HELPS

DEVELOP

your

SKILLS

Medieval, Gothic, & Blackletter

Want a fresh approach to traditional writing styles? Medieval and Gothic styles of hand-lettering combine the best aspects of traditional and ontemporary styles. These themes conjure up images of ancient wonders, nights, and grand castles! Today when you think of Medieval style, you think of eavy ornamentation and of all the trappings of that knightly era, while when ou think of Gothic style, you think of books and films that describe strange and ometimes frightening events, often in mysterious and spooky places. Gothic ften has overtones of horror, vampires, and dark forests filled with strange oises and shapes. It is great fun to take a contemporary lettering approach to hese types of old-fashioned styles, so what are you waiting for? Find out what 's all about and start creating elaborate artworks to impress your friends!

Medieval

Medieval script was common from the 4th to the th centuries. Originally used by Greek and Latin vriters, over time it was taken up by Irish and nglish writers too. Variations on this style came ater (some of which developed into the Gothic tyle). You may have seen this style in illuminated or decorated) manuscripts found in old Bibles and rayer books, but these days it continues to appear n elegant signs and advertising. It also works well vith Gothic-style lettering, since both were created vith similar tools hundreds of years ago.

Gothic

othic lettering was the main lettering style of the Middle Ages, prevailing from roughly 1200–1500. he term "Gothic" originated with the Italians, who sed it to refer to what they saw as barbarian ultures to the North of their borders! Gothic covers nany early handwriting styles: some are expressive vith lots of curves and smooth corners while thers are more angular with hard, straight lines nd precise angles. You can see this traditional, ld-fashioned style used for attention-grabbing ontrast on advertisements for super-modern roducts. But above all, it's just beautiful to look at.

Blackletter

A sub-style of Gothic is called Blackletter; it's named that because the visual weight of the lettering is so heavy that it crowds out the white space on a page. This style was particularly popular in Germany in the Middle Ages. We've chosen Blackletter as a style of Gothic to focus on because it has made a comeback in recent years, with young designers finding unexpected uses for traditional lettering in contemporary artwork and media.

In this chapter we are going to learn some fun ways to incorporate these styles into your own hand-lettering designs.

Medieval

Here is a full Medieval alphabet that you can copy or trace.
There is space provided on the opposite page to practice.

ABCDEFGHI
JKLMNOP
QRSTUVW
XYZ &?!
abcdefghij
klmnopqrs
tuvwxyz

Olde Worlde

This first project gets you into the old-fashioned spirit with a traditionally lettered Medieval-style phrase set into a simple circle.

1. Draw a circle using a compass or stencil. Alternatively, draw around a can or small plate. Sketch baseline and horizontal guidelines to keep your letter-height consistent and vertical guidelines to keep your verticals straight. Then, instead of doing just a single line for your letter skeleton, roughly hatch along this line (that means adding fine, parallel lines drawn closely together) as shown, to provide a sense of each letterform's shape and how much space it should take up. This is a useful method for these styles and will be used throughout the section. For this design we will also use flourishes to fill in the circle outline. There are lots of extravagant flourishes that you can make but they can be quite tricky, so at the beginning you may want to trace them from our circle.

2. Start by sketching an outline on your rough letter shapes, then add thick and thin strokes at the ends of your flourishes—known (unsurprisingly!) as "thicks" and "thins" respectively. For this design, make the thicks a little chunkier and more dramatic in comparison to the thins. Also try really rounding your d's and e's on their left edge for a more Medieval effect.

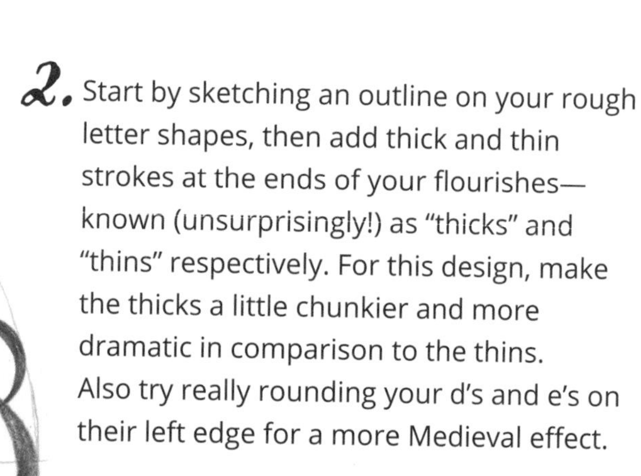

3. Finalize your drawing by using a pen or marker to ink over your sketch. Erase any pencil lines when dry. Alternatively, you can copy the lettering onto tracing paper first. This is an option for any of the projects. It allows you to use the tracing paper lettering as a template for future use, or to transfer them immediately onto a separate piece of paper.

Oh, What a Knight!

Now we are getting more ambitious with a cheeky phrase and a more complicated composition. Take a deep breath, stay calm, and ready your pencil lance for lettering victory!

1. Draw your horizontal and vertical guidelines. Then hatch your letters and look for opportunities to draw flourishes from your letterforms. Start simple with triangular serifs on top of your main letter strokes. For this design, make the flourishes circular and tightly drawn for an added ornate effect.

2. Now use a softer (darker) lead pencil to start fleshing out the lettering. Let's add a few points at the tops of the letters and drop down the right leg of both h's so they come to a sharp point. Extend the g as in the example and add some expansive curves to the W and K. No need to add different weights (thicks and thins) to the flourishes: we will stick with a basic monoweight line for this design.

3. Now that you have a detailed outline, finalize your drawing by using a pen or marker to ink over your sketch, and erase any pencil lines. Keep your flourish lines clean and light, and emphasize the pointed ends on the letters.

Illuminated Letter

A fun Medieval-style hand-lettering project is to create an illuminated (or decorated) letter. Hand-lettering an elaborate capital letter, usually for the first letter of a page or paragraph, was a Medieval custom that you can still see in books, like traditional fairy tales. These letters were elaborately decorated with interwoven patterns and pictures, which were used to embellish and brighten manuscripts.

1. Draw a square box. Sketch in a letter A in Medieval style, making it fill most of the square. When you are happy with your letter, start playing around with flourishes. These decorations need to feel like flowers and plants growing through, across, and around the letter.

2. Start filling in your flourishes. You can look at pictures of flowers and leaves to find inspiration for decorating your letters. Vary the thickness of the decoration, remembering to keep your lines loose and relaxed.

3. Finalize your drawing by using a pen or marker to ink over your sketch. Instead of filling in the vines and the letters, fill in the background. This will make the white letter and flourishes really stand out against the surrounding black space. Ink in the square border around your design. See how awesome the white design looks against the black background with a strong black border!

Try illuminating the first letter of your name!

TIP

The stark effect of white against black looks amazing, but you can also experiment with color. Medieval illuminated letters also used gold and other rich colors against a darker background, so experiment with different colored markers on these letters. Or, to really shine, use metallics like gold or silver!

There are many different styles of illuminated letters that vary throughout history and across different cultures. Often they depict dramatic line patterns, plants, animals, and mythological creatures. We've included some examples here to inspire you.

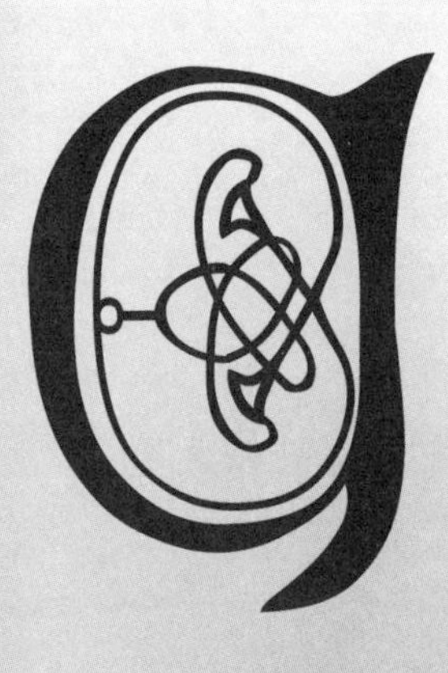

Now try creating some of your own!

Here is a full Blackletter alphabet that you can copy or trace.
There is space provided on the opposite page to practice.

ABCDEFG
HIJKLMN
OPQRSTU
VWXYZ&?!

abcdefghij
klmnopqrs
tuvwxyz

Carpe Diem

"Seize the Day!" Horace, the famous Roman poet, penned these words in 23 BCE, well before the Gothic script was in use, but this inspirational saying is still true today and is a great way to introduce this new outlined version of Blackletter.

1. Draw a template of guidelines to help you sketch out the design. Roughly hatch your Blackletter letters by sketching diagonal lines as if you were filling in an outline. Now look out for opportunities to draw flourishes off the letterforms. You'll be surprised at how many awesome flourishes you can pack in once you start looking. Avoid congestion by keeping your flourishes open and smooth.

2. Sketch an outline around your rough letter shapes and add thicks and thins to the ends of your flourishes. The subtitle translation should contrast with the main phrase, so let's dress it up a little! The design doesn't have to be this complicated —you can keep it simple and outline the swirly border, or allow just a flourish or two to come off the D and C.

3. As you're filling in the letterforms with ink, leave small bars of white space in the letters to give it a more decorative look. This lightens the look of the piece and gives it a more stylish touch. Finalize your drawing by using a pen or marker to ink over your sketch and erase any pencil marks.

This design is in the Old English style of Blackletter, which is sharper and more angular than other kinds of Blackletter. Historically this Old English style signifies strength and courage, especially as represented by knights and warriors.

1. Start by sketching the outline of your shield shape, then draw in guidelines to help as you progress. Notice how the curved letters give the piece strength and also work well within the shape of the shield itself. As you letter, you should come across some opportunities to include a few tasteful flourishes. You can even include a little symbol, like the simplified fleur-de-lis ("flower of the lily") included here at the bottom of the shield, as further decoration.

2. Sketch an outline around your rough letter shapes and add thicks and thins to your flourishes.

3. Finalize your drawing by using a pen or marker to ink over your sketch and create the final shield artwork.

Strong And Brave

Create your own knight's shield!

The Brothers Grimm

The Brothers Grimm were two brothers who published *Kinder- und Hausmärchen* (*Children's and Household Tales*), a collection of over 200 fairy tales that has become one of the most influential works in the world. This book was printed in the early 19th century but the tales they collected are much, much older. The stories are also quite dark with overtones of horror, which definitely fits the use of Gothic script as the main feature of this design to act as a tribute to their work!

1. Draw an overall rectangular guideline and the letter base-lines to help you as you sketch. You'll notice there is an arc shape for the top "TALES FROM," a wavy banner-style shape for "Brothers" and straight parallel lines for "The" and "Grimm." In this design we'll be working with Gothic and Medieval lettering. Use the Medieval alphabet for "TALES FROM" and the letter shapes of the Blackletter alphabet for "The Brothers Grimm," but make the letterforms thinner and lighter for this alternative Gothic style. Start by hatching in your curved Gothic text. Then look for opportunities to draw some flourishes to frame your letterforms, like the example.

2. Sketch an outline around your rough letter shapes and add thicks and thins to your flourishes. Your flourishes can overlap, as they do over the m of "Grimm," but just make sure your composition is still clear enough to read.

3. Finalize your drawing by using a pen or marker to ink over your sketch, and erase any pencil marks.

Now with Grimm determination, have a go!

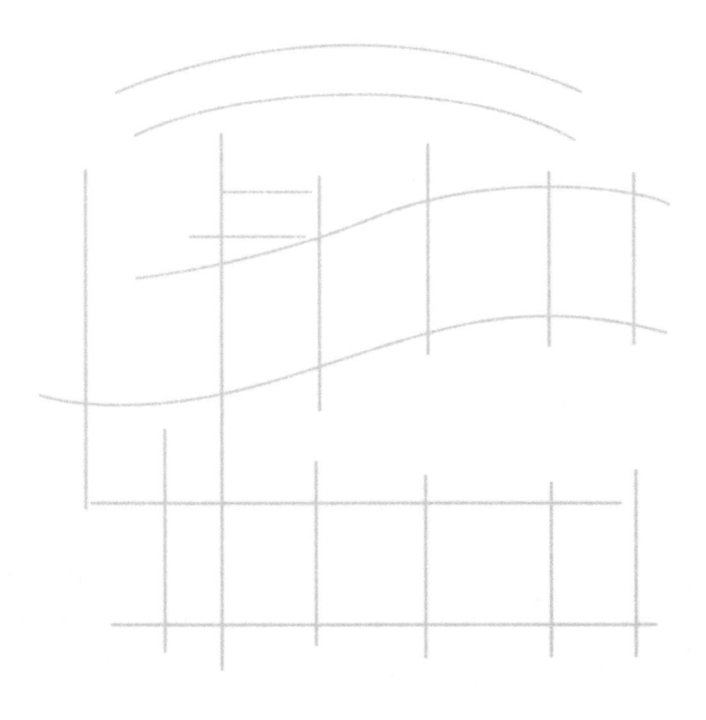

The Sword in the Stone

"Whoso pulleth out this sword of this stone and anvil, is rightwise King born of all England." According to 15th-century English writer Thomas Malory, thus Arthur discovered he was Uther Pendragon's heir, destined to become king! This fabled event gives us an epic chance to practice our Gothic lettering.

1. This is a more advanced project where the words are contained within an invisible circle. This type of design is more like a puzzle and requires careful planning to get everything to fit. As usual, draw your guidelines first.

TIP

Always have a hard-lead and a soft-lead pencil at hand. Hard lead creates a softer pencil line that is great for early guidelines and sketches, while soft lead provides a darker pencil line that is excellent for more developed artwork.

2. Now that you have sketched your rough letterforms and flourishes, use a softer (darker) lead pencil to add thicks and thins to the flourishes. Use this opportunity to smooth out the letter shapes and make them fit comfortably with each other. Make both S's feel bold and strong in the design and try interlocking the flourishes into the lettering. Rub out and redraw as often as necessary until you get it absolutely right.

3. Now that you have a detailed sketch, finalize your drawing by using a pen or marker to ink over your sketch, and erase any pencil marks. It should feel bold and ornate—a good mixture of royal power and its accompanying decorative royal pomp!

The Sword In The Stone

Now it's your turn to take on this quest!

Blackletter type can be seen in headings, logos, posters, and signs. It is often used for official certificates or diplomas, giving them a feeling of age and importance. You may have seen Blackletter-style fonts used for newspaper mastheads, in a similar style to the examples below.

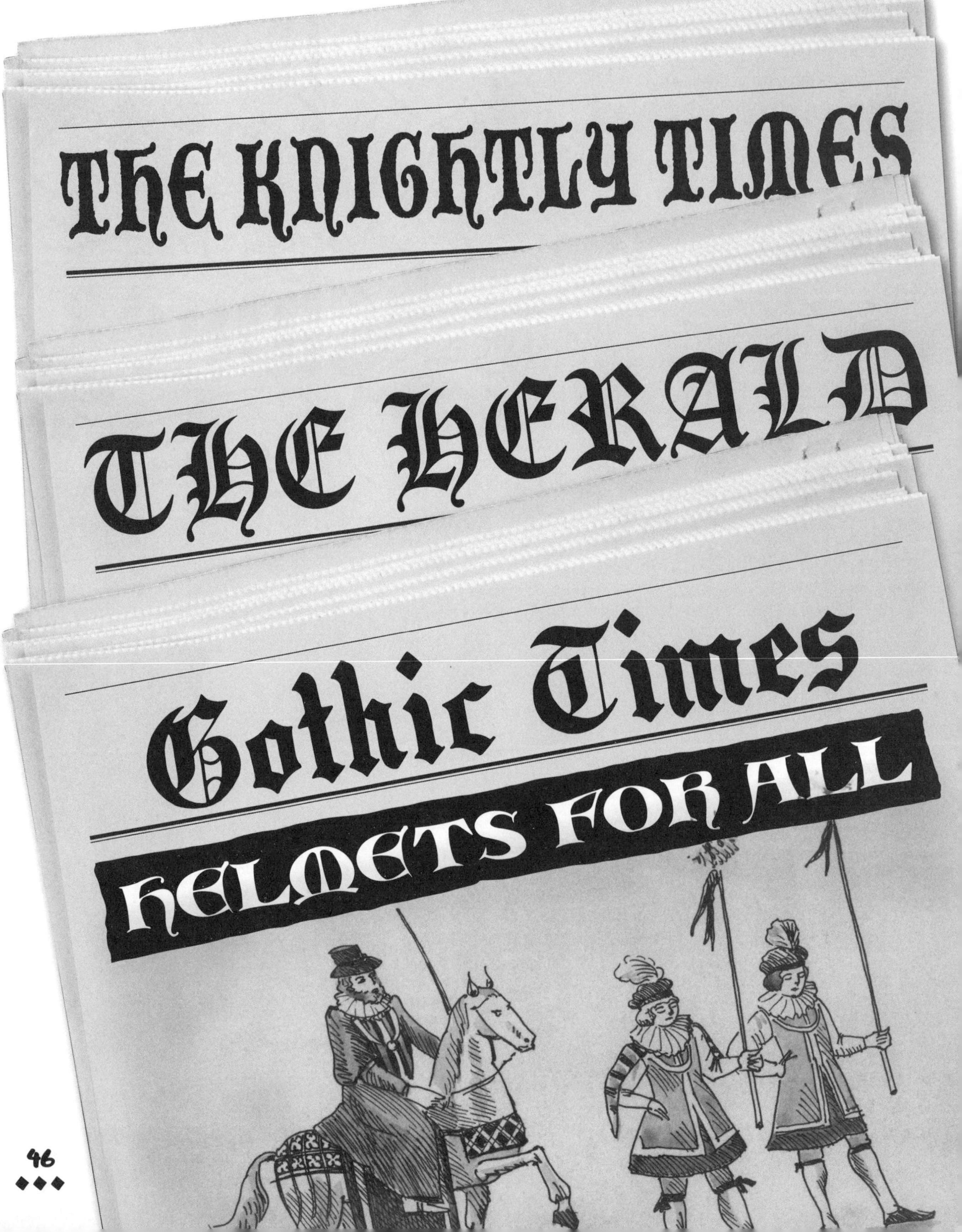

THE KNIGHTLY TIMES

THE HERALD

Gothic Times

HELMETS FOR ALL

Jsing the templates below, create your own newspaper mastheads
or your family, school, or team!

Congratulations! You are well on the way to becoming a master Medieval and Gothic hand-letterer. You need to be as ornate as possible with these styles, so keep experimenting and practicing, and let your imagination run riot! Just remember:

Vintage & Retro

The old-fashioned quality of these letter styles is mostly associated with the elegance of times gone by and instantly brings to mind much simpler times. Broadly speaking, Vintage lettering dates from the mid-19th century—the Victorian age—while Retro lettering tends to refer to the styles that evolved in the mid-20th century.

Vintage

In the 1800s mass-produced commercial products became common. One of the ways manufacturers attracted attention was how they presented their goods. Ornate lettering styles therefore beautified everything from soap packaging to tea tins. The letters themselves became the artwork, and were often embellished with beautifully scrolled and extended serifs. Stores became filled with wonderfully artistic and tempting products.

The Showboat alphabet we'll explore brings to mind Victorian stores, Western saloons, fairgrounds and circuses, and old-fashioned entertainment like long-disappeared music halls. It's great for dropped capitals (the large letter sometimes used at the beginning of text, like the first letter on this page) or on signs or notices.

This section will explore some of these beautiful hand-lettering styles, which you can apply to your own artistic creations for a cool Vintage feel.

Retro

In time, designers grew tired of fussy Vintage lettering and looked for a cleaner, more modern style, which we now refer to as "Retro." This type of lettering embodies all the fun of the 1950s and '60s when everything American was exciting and modern.

You can feel this sensation through hand-lettering too, as shown in the styles in this section. For instance, Signpainter is an alphabet that embodies all the fun of the 1950s. It's a really optimistic style: gently curved capitals convey movement and hopeful expectations and lowercase letters display a fresh and cheerful attitude. It looks fantastic on menus and advertisements.

The exuberance of 1950s lettering mellowed into more polished styles in the following decade, but still kept a merry mood. Sophisticated yet playful, the Jazz alphabet explored in this section captures the essence of the early 1960s. Refined letterforms are tilted for a touch of whimsy with punchy, oversized capitals bringing to mind modern architecture, fin-tailed cars, cocktail parties, swirling petticoat dresses, and sharp-suited businessmen. Use this style of lettering when you want some elegance and sophistication with a touch of American glamor: try it on invitations and event signs!

Showboat

Here is a full Vintage alphabet, called Showboat, that you can copy or trace for practice. There is space on the opposite page to practice.

ABCDEFG

HIJKLMN

OPQRSTU

VWXYZ

?!&

Fine Antiques

Try out the vintage Showboat alphabet style with an old-fashioned sign featuring a pointing hand. The look is unmistakably from olden times so it's ideal for anything that deals with the Victorian past (such as antiques). Or try adapting this sign for a costume party, with the finger pointing the way to the fun!

1. Draw a rectangle and add two sets of guidelines for your letters. Sketch a border around the rectangle and then round off the corners.

TIP

This project uses a design element called a "spur": a small point or projection that comes off the main part of a letter. It gives this script a cool Victorian feel!

2. Write the word "FINE" in the upper left of the rectangle. Sketch (or trace) a pointing hand in the space in the top right. Add small lines on the hand to make it resemble an old-fashioned woodcut. Center "ANTIQUES" below.

FINE ANTIQUES

3. Ink your design by carefully going over your pencil marks with a nib pen. When this is finished and dry, gently erase the pencil marks. Lastly, outline the border around the text.

Now we've pointed the way,
it's your turn to make your own olde-timey sign!

Letter Love

Now it's time to really go all out with decorating your letters. Because of their Vintage look, these letters offer loads of scope for imaginative old-fashioned embellishments and frills.

1. Sketch two sets of guidelines. Write "LETTER" at the top and "LOVE" centered beneath. With all the letters except V, place the spurs on the letter stems so they are intersected by the center guideline.

2. Erase unnecessary lines inside the words so you have a clean area for embellishing.

3. Get creative! Add ropes, jewels, feathers, and other fun flourishes to your letters. You could add flowers, fruit, and vines, or fill the center of the letters with patterns such as stripes or dots.

TIP

Be careful not to lose the shape of the letters with over-enthusiastic embellishments outside the edges.

4. When you are satisfied with your design, ink it in. Fill the various elements but leave some space empty for contrast. Try adding shadows to some of the letters. When this is finished and dry, erase any pencil marks. This type of lettering also looks gorgeous in color. Feeling fancy? Ink some elements using a metallic gold or silver pen!

LETTER LOVE

Have a go at creating your own lovely letters!

Add embellishments to your letters, like on the first two examples below. Try experimenting with the other letters by adding your own designs, filling them in with all sorts of extra details. You could add flourishes, embellishments, shadows, patterns, highlights, shaped borders, or even illustrations to your letters. Let your imagination run wild!

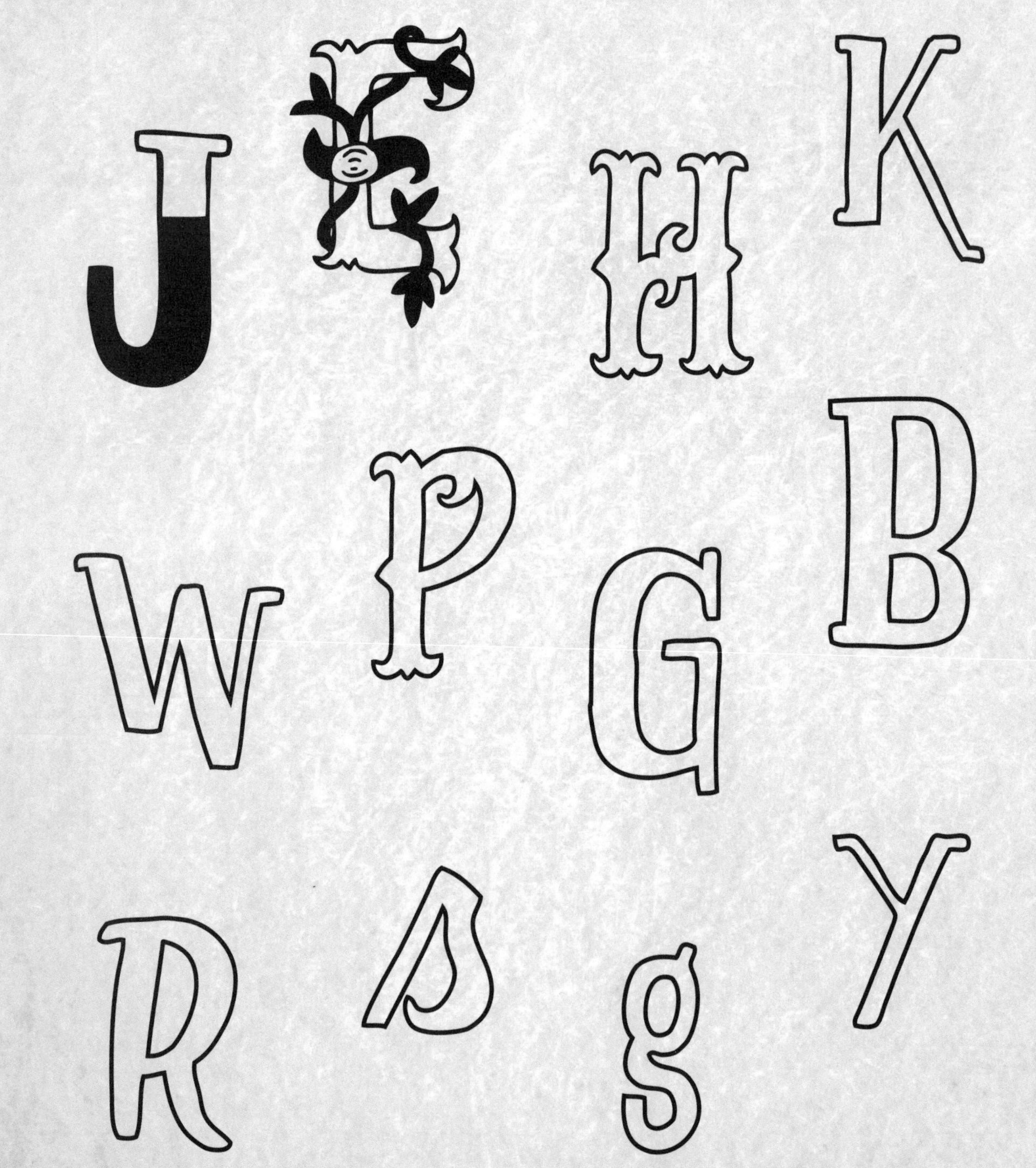

In this space you can draw your own letters and decorate them. Go mad and fill up the space with your own amazing creations!

Signpainter

Here is a full Retro alphabet, called Signpainter, that you can copy or trace.
There is space provided on the opposite page to practice.

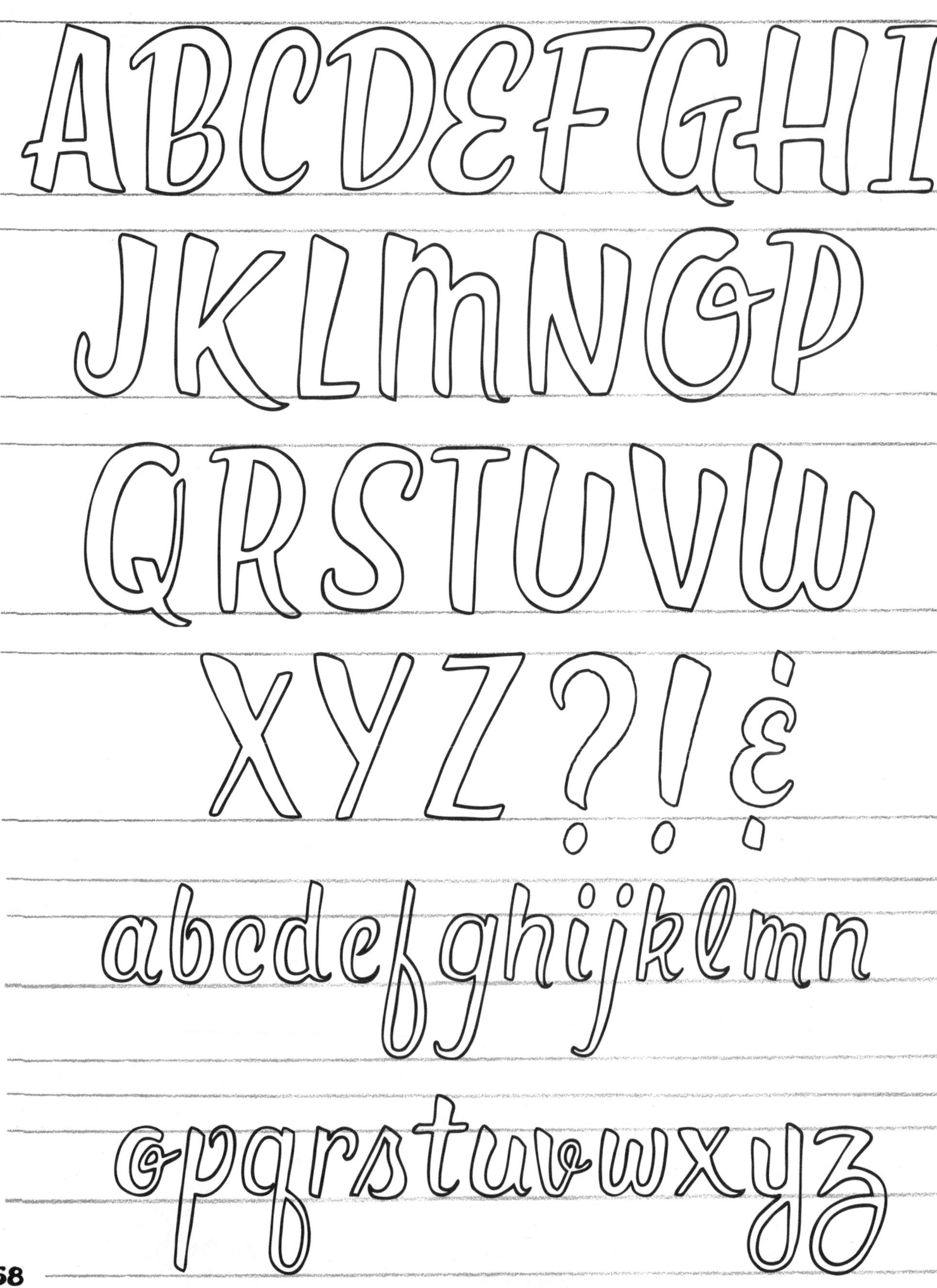

Donuts & Coffee

This project uses the Signpainter hand-lettering style to evoke an American diner, and what says this better than donuts? Work your Retro lettering in an imaginary circle to echo its shape.

1. Sketch a large circle (use a compass if you want precision) and add a smaller center circle to turn it into a donut. Add a wavy ring of frosting on top and a scattering of rectangular sprinkles. Add diagonal shading lines from the frosting to the edge of the donut ring.

2. Create two sets of guidelines that follow the curves of the donut for the lettering above and below the image. Sketch the word "DONUTS" at the top and "COFFEE" at the bottom.

3. Draw a ribbon banner curling across the donut by sketching two slightly curved bands on the left and right sides of the donut. Draw a band that bends slightly upward to connect each side in the hole. To create the ends of the ribbon, draw extensions to each side, slightly lower than where the ribbon sections sit on the donut, and add a triangular notch to each end to finish. Add shading lines to the ribbon where it curves over the donut to give the impression of depth.

Sketch "hot" on the left of the banner and "fresh" on the right. Add a big ampersand (&: the symbol for "and") in the center of the donut hole. Add wedge-shaped accents in the white space around the donut.

4. Finalize your drawing by using a pen or marker to ink over your sketch. When this is finished and dry, erase any pencil marks. Alternatively, copy it onto tracing paper. Add stipple shading (lots of tiny dots) on the segments of banner that are "behind" the donut.

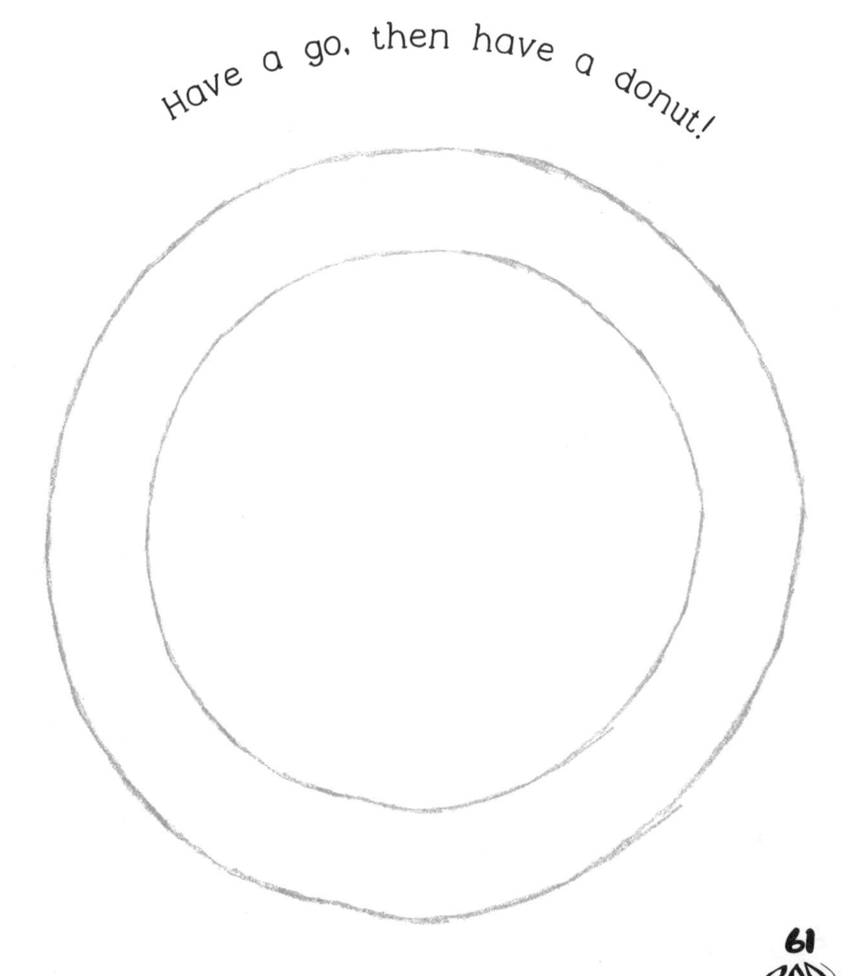

J's Diner

Let's work at something a little more complicated and sophisticated for this Signpainter style: a 1950s-style diner sign incorporating several different shapes. This time the lettering and the image are inextricably linked, and while this looks simple, it still takes some careful thought to create.

1. Start by sketching a jelly-bean shape. Then add a series of five trapezoids (triangles without the top peak), alternating between pointing up and down in orientation.

Make an arrow sign by drawing a rectangle across the top of the trapezoids and a second rectangle with an arrowhead pointing down on the right side. Sketch in guidelines for your letters as needed.

2. Why not personalize this project by adding your own initial on top of the rectangle? Using the Signpainter style, make this letter quite large followed by an apostrophe and a smaller s. Write the word "DINER" within the trapezoids. As you finish sections, you can start erasing guidelines you don't need anymore, like the ones that go through the arrow.

3. Add "open late!" in lowercase Signpainter script underneath the word "DINER." Fill in the blank areas with retro accents, like these asterisk flourishes that have a circle in the middle and at the end of each line.

Draw a border within the arrow sign and add a series of circular lights, reminiscent of the glowing light bulbs often found in 1950s neon signs.

4. Ink your design and erase any pencil marks when dry. Try filling in the background of the trapezoids while leaving the letters white for contrast. Apply this to your flourishes too, for a balanced finish.

Now it's your turn to create some sign art!

Let's Get Creative!

Choose an object you love and hand-letter a word or phrase on it using the Signpainter script and decorations. The object can be anything that you are able to write on: for example a pencil case or a notebook. You could even buy a porcelain cup and paint on it. Personalizing your designs would also make the perfect gifts for your friends and family! Use this practice space to perfect your designs before copying them onto your object.

but
first,
COFFEE

Jazz

Here is a full Retro alphabet, known as Jazz, that you can copy or trace.
There is space provided on the opposite page to practice.

ABCDEFGHIJ

KLMNOPQRST

UVWXYZ?!&

abcdefghijklmn

opqrstuvwxyz

Golden Goose Jazz Club

Welcome to the club! The look is Retro: clean and simple but with some drama created by using lowercase lettering for the club's name and capitals for the type of venue. This type of sign would also look brilliant for your sports club!

1. Sketch out your guidelines and write "golden goose" in the lowercase Jazz alphabet. Write "JAZZ CLUB" beneath "golden goose." Alternate the position of the letters above and below the baseline to give them a sense of movement. Extend the leg of the A to touch the lowest guideline. Note how the B in this script is top-heavy.

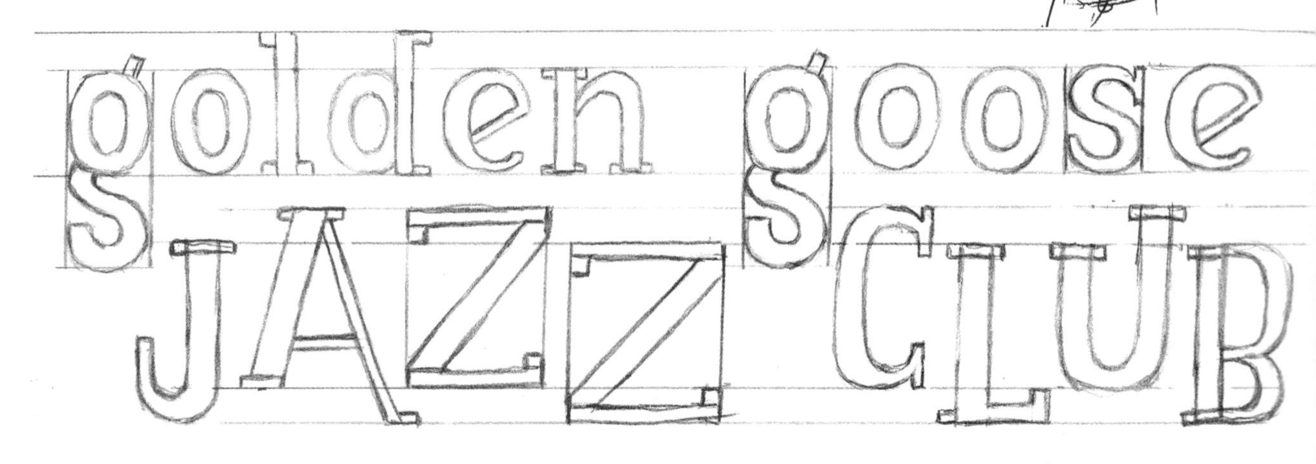

TIP

It may be helpful to draw the tricky gs in "golden goose" within two equal rectangles to get the correct proportions.

2. Sketch a rectangular border around the text and round off the corners. Add a second border outside the first one. Draw a music note in the empty space beside the J.

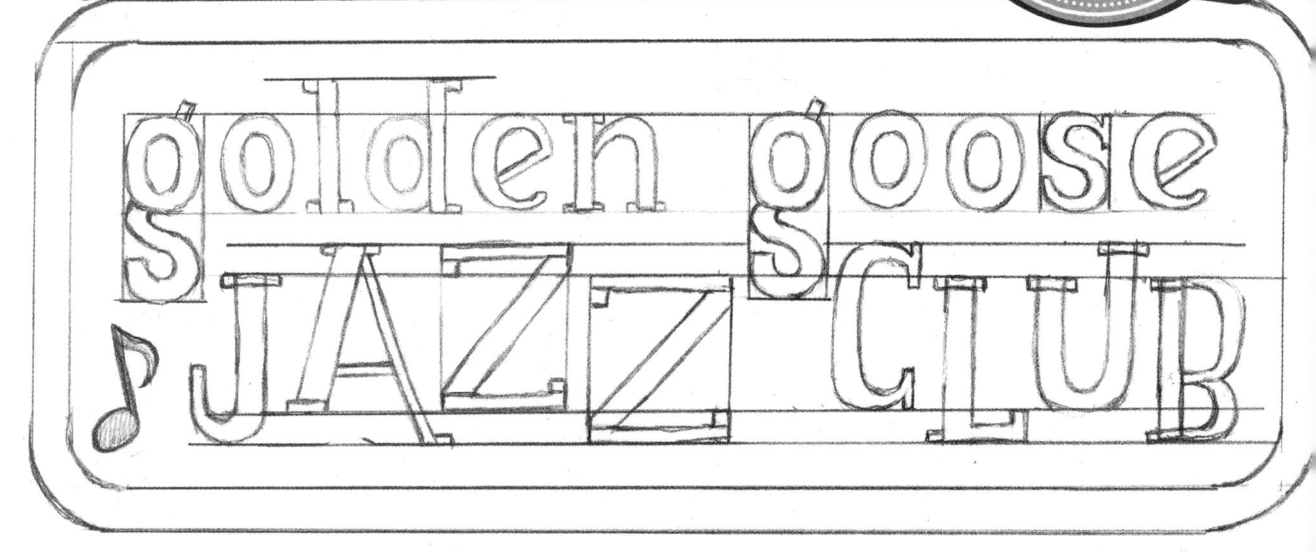

3. Finalize your drawing by using a pen or marker to ink over your sketch, then erase any pencil marks when dry. Alternatively, copy it onto tracing paper. Try leaving a white shine or reflection mark on the upper left-hand curves of the lowercase letters. Consider coloring in only half of each capital letterform for a playful vibe. Finally, fill in the border, leaving a few shiny white stripes.

golden goose
JAZZ CLUB

Now let's make some lettering harmonies!

Love You to the Moon and Back

For this project using the Jazz script, the words need to work well with the illustration. This design looks really cool with the eye of the moon sitting inside the letter E.

1. Begin by drawing a pair of clouds. If you find these tricky, draw half an oval, then sketch bumps along the outside of the shape. Add a full moon behind the clouds and a couple of diamond-shaped stars.

2. "LOVE" and "MOON" are the key words in this piece, so start by drawing their guidelines. Sketch in the word "MOON" near the bottom of the cloud, ranging the letters up and down. Then use the lowercase alphabet to write "and back" in smaller letters to the right. Write "you" above the M of the word "MOON" and "the" above the N.

3. Write the word "to" slanting upward between "you" and "the." Draw a small rectangle around it and turn it into a banner by adding a rectangle to the left and right sides, notching a v shape at each end. Add the word "LOVE" at the top, again staggering the letters.

4. Finalize your drawing by using a pen or marker to ink over your sketch, then erase any pencil marks. Alternatively, copy it onto tracing paper. Fill in the letters with black ink so they are easy to see against the illustration. Add texture to the drawing elements by adding stippled dots, lines, or crosshatching.

TIP

If you want to combine lettering and illustration, make sure that your drawing doesn't overwhelm your letters.

LOVE you to the MOON and back

Now it's your turn!

You'll be over the moon when you create this amazing design!

Project Inspiration

Transform the look and feel of any lettering style by adding shadows. Also, try using swooping flourishes to accent your vintage design.

Calligraphy- & Brush- Style Scripts

Learning the art of calligraphy takes years, regardless of whether it's with a brush or a pen. But that doesn't mean we can't draw inspiration from the masters to create our own versions! In this section, you will learn how to draw script in a way that is organic, fun, and easy to read, without needing to use specialized pens and brushes.

The common element between these scripts is loose, free, and effortless movement—or the semblance of it. Another key aspect of these styles is personality: everyone's handwriting is different, and this difference adds individuality to your lettering. Both of these qualities are expressed in the two styles of this section: brush-style and calligraphy hand-lettering scripts.

Brush-Style Script

Brush-style script is a common and popular form of hand-lettering. It is often used to announce a celebration or advertise a big event, like a sale. The look is bold and loud as well as stylish and smooth. Brush-style hand-lettering is especially attractive because it is personal: each artist draws brush script differently, so it is often a style that mirrors the artist's personality.

Calligraphy-Style Script

Calligraphy means different things to different people: beautiful copperplate handwriting, the elegant brushstrokes of Japanese masters, or the smooth-flowing script of a signwriter. Calligraphy is closely related to handwriting and is usually produced with a brush or a broad-tip pen, but its style can be simulated through pencil and regular pens as well. The calligraphic style that emulates nib-based calligraphy looks a bit more formal and controlled than brush-style lettering. Calligraphy hand-lettering scripts are great for special cards and invitations, journaling, displayable lettering artworks, and celebratory projects like banners or certificates.

Brush-Style Script

Here is a full Brush-style-script alphabet that you can copy or trace.
There is space on the opposite page to practice.

Aa Bb Cc Dd Ee

Ff Gg Hh Ii Jj

Kk Ll Mm Nn

Oo Pp Qq Rr Ss

Tt Uu Vv Ww

Xx Yy Zz !?&

My Brilliant Ideas!

Brush-style script isn't as structured as other hand-lettering styles. It is meant to look like it has been casually written using a brush, although it can actually be created with a pen. The result should look smooth and effortless. Just remember to keep your lettering loose and organic. For this project, we will be doing a vertical-brush script. Keep your lines loose and don't worry if they're not perfect—it adds to the individuality and fun of the piece!

1. Start by drawing your guidelines, then sketch a basic brush script outline. Make the vertical stems thick and juicy with smooth curves while keeping the lines that join the letters and the lines at the ends of the letters thin and elegant. Try to think of the lines as one continuous brushstroke per word. Then add a burst of lines around your design to create the impression of an explosive idea!

2. Fill in your letterforms. Check that the composition is easy to read and that the letters are even and balanced across the composition. Erase anything and adjust it as needed.

TIP
Play around with different decoration styles to draw attention to your lettering. Sometimes a burst of lines around your lettering can make all the difference between an exciting design and a boring one!

3. Using your detailed sketch (or a copy that you have made on tracing paper), trace over the letters with a pen or marker and erase any pencil marks. Use your draft as a guide but don't worry about following it exactly, as you want to keep your lines loose and organic. You can also experiment with a brush-pen or a marker to fill in the strokes.

Now it's your turn to create this brilliant project! Remember: develop your own brush style, stay loose, and embrace your individual look!

The Ice Cream Shop

Retro-style brush script immediately conjures up the energy and excitement of the 1950s and '60s. It evokes ice-cream parlors and roadside diners, where teens listen to rock 'n' roll on the jukebox while sharing a milkshake with two straws. This project expresses that nostalgic energy with its retro, fluid brush style.

1. First, draw a rectangle. Then draw diagonal parallel guidelines across the middle, so that the letters will be the same height and slanted at the same angle. Quickly draw a natural single-line script, keeping within the guidelines. This simple sketch is the foundation for your brush script.

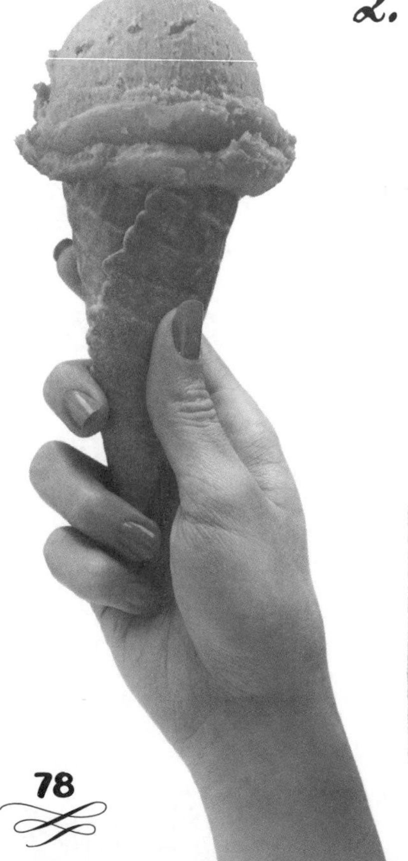

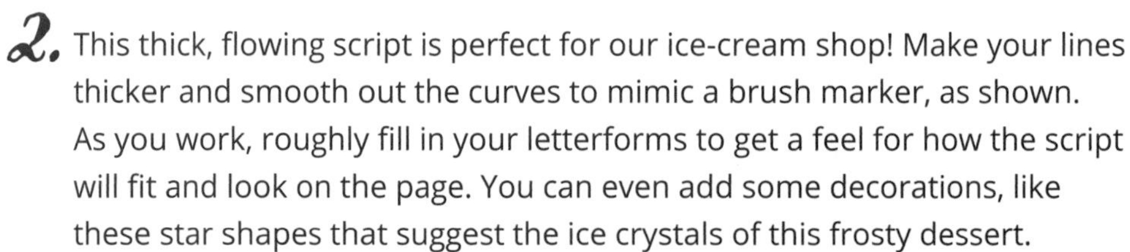

2. This thick, flowing script is perfect for our ice-cream shop! Make your lines thicker and smooth out the curves to mimic a brush marker, as shown. As you work, roughly fill in your letterforms to get a feel for how the script will fit and look on the page. You can even add some decorations, like these star shapes that suggest the ice crystals of this frosty dessert.

3. Now that you have a detailed sketch, ink over it with a pen or marker and erase any pencil marks. Alternatively, copy it onto tracing paper to to avoid any stubborn remaining sketch marks and to transfer to a fresh piece of paper. You can even use this tracing-paper copy to use as a template for future designs. You can do this for all of these projects in this section.

Now it's your turn to create this cool blast from the past!

Let's Get Creative!

Using the two brush-script lettering styles you've just learned, letter a list of your favorite ice-cream flavors in a flowing, drippy ice-cream design. Why not try decorating them in the style of your favorite flavors too?

Strawberry

Chocolate

I scream,
you scream,
we all scream
for ice cream!

A Brush with Greatness

Brush-style script is flexible and adaptable. It works when used loosely or, as here, with a more structured approach. In this more formal-looking exercise, we're using a symmetrical structure: emphasizing the important words but also adding contrasting flourishes to the less important words. This composition combines a casual upright brush script, a single-stroke italic script, and an all-caps brush script.

1. Draw guidelines and sketch in your letters, keeping them loose and natural. Take time to work out your letter width, letter spacing, and word shape. Draw "with" as a simple, single-line italic script. Try adding a little flourish to the crossbar of the A and to the leg of the R in "GREATNESS."

2. Sketch out thick and thin strokes at the ends of your flourishes (known as thicks and thins) for each style. Add a little weight around the right vertical stem of the A to give the script an elegant look. Try sketching thicker, juicier stems to give the word "Brush" a chunkier feel. "GREATNESS" is emphasized by using thick vertical stems and thin contrasting lines.

3. Now that you have an awesome sketch, finalize your drawing by using a pen or marker to ink over your work, then erase any pencil marks once the ink is dry.

A Brush with GREATNESS

Try this triple-decker brush script yourself!

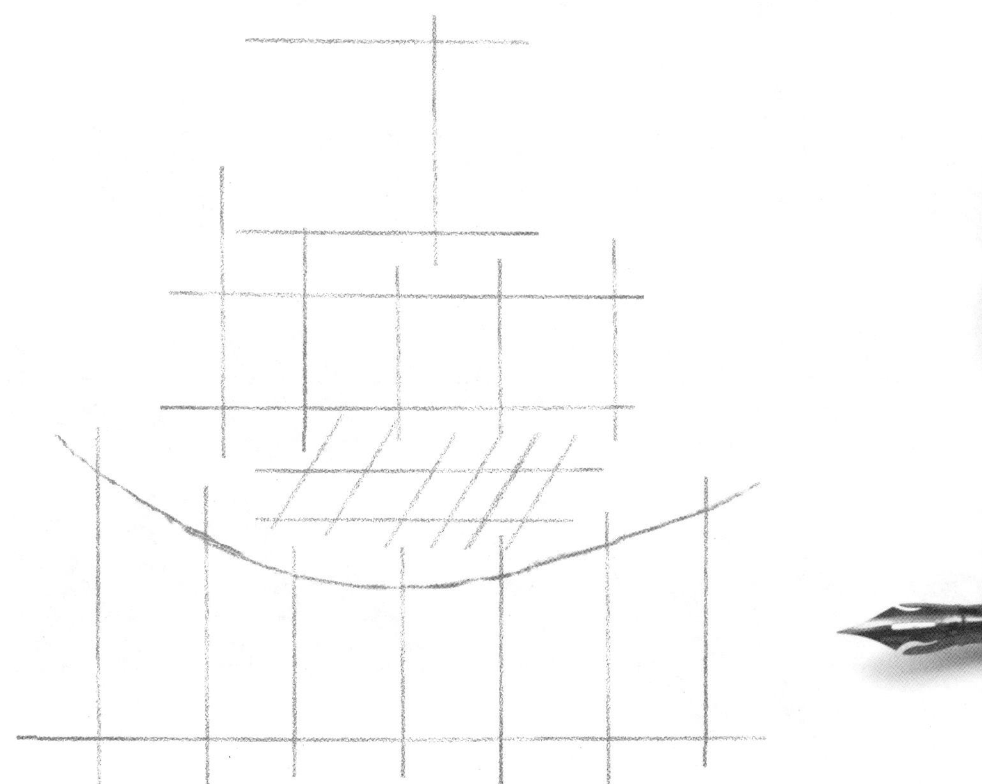

Calligraphy-Style Script

Here is a full calligraphy alphabet that you can copy or trace for practice.
There is space on the opposite page to practice.

Aa Bb Cc Dd

Ee Ff Gg Hh

Ii Jj Kk Ll

Mm Nn Oo

Pp Qq Rr Ss

Tt Uu Vv Ww

Xx Yy Zz ! ? &

Congrats!

Let's now turn our focus to calligraphy-style script, a more formal and elegant type of lettering than brush-style script. This is a version of a refined Elizabethan-style calligraphic hand-lettering script, based on styles from around the 16th century. Enjoy its regal elegance!

1. Draw two parallel curved lines to set the height and shape of your script and add a few slanted parallel guidelines so that the angle of your script is consistent. Sketch out a nice single-pencil-stroke script to get your spacing and letter-width proportions worked out. Next, look for opportunities to add flourishes coming off the letterforms. See what kinds of flourishes you can add—take particular note of the g and the crossbar on the t. Erase and revise as needed while you work this out.

2. To make this script look more dramatic yet refined, sketch out thicker stems on your letters to contrast with the thinner lines of the connecting strokes and flourishes. Make sure your stems come to a smooth point at the bottom before curving up and connecting to the next letter: these transitions should look seamless. Fill in the letters as you go, making sure they are easy to read.

3. Finish your drawing by using a pen or marker to ink over your sketch and erase any pencil marks when dry.

TIP

Play with your thicks and thins to achieve different effects. For instance, sharper terminals (or the ends of a stroke without a serif) make for a more refined script. On the other hand, expressive, chunkier lines produce a more casual style.

You'll be congratulating yourself when you complete this lettering!

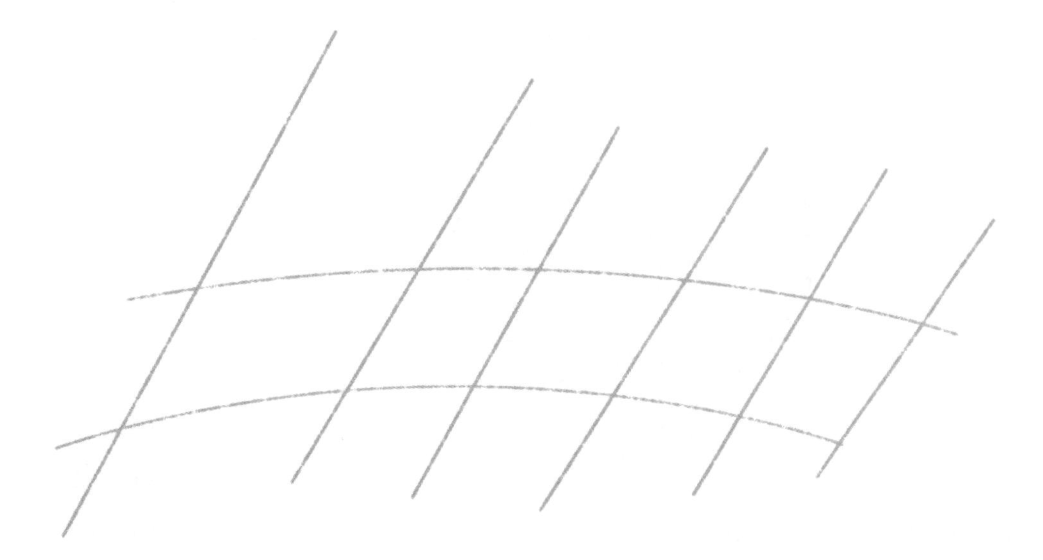

Calligraphy looks great on gift tags; it's an elegant way to convey messages without being overly formal. Adding a hand-lettered gift tag enhances and personalizes any birthday present or special gift! Using these templates, create designs for any upcoming events you may have.

With joy

With Love

TO: ____________________

FROM: ____________________

Decorate these tags as much or as little as you want—they're your creations!

Have fun creating your own unique gift tags for the special people in your life!

Sugar and Spice

For this project we will be combining a beautifully sweet calligraphic script with a spicy and vibrant lettering style for dramatic visual effect.

1. Draw the guidelines as illustrated by drawing straight parallel lines for "Sugar" and curved lines for "SPICE." For "Sugar" you may want to draw some rough diagonal lines on which to center each slanted letter. Also make sure you leave enough for &. Now let's sketch your lettering. Draw a simple single-line script of the word "Sugar" and then draw the word "SPICE" in a natural upright style along the curve. Sketch in the ampersand (&). Try adding your own flourishes off the letters g and s in "Sugar" and the &. Erase and redraw until you're happy with your work. Finally, add a few explosive lines coming off the word "SPICE" for added effect.

2. The top script should feel sweet as sugar, so sketch in some smooth lines to thicken up the letters, as in the example. Keep the tops rounded and the transitions from the thick to thin strokes super smooth. Add some weight to the flourishes of the g. Sketch in thicker stems for the word "SPICE" to contrast with the thins.

3. Now smooth out the "Sugar" script and the ampersand. Instead of drawing smooth clean lines around the word "SPICE," make the letter edges jagged so that they resemble wavy lines of heat, like a chili! Do the same with the lines coming off this word. Erase and re-sketch as needed until you are happy with your hand-lettering.

4. Finish your drawing by using a pen or marker to ink over your sketch, and erase any pencil marks when the ink is dry. Your dynamic concoction is ready to serve!

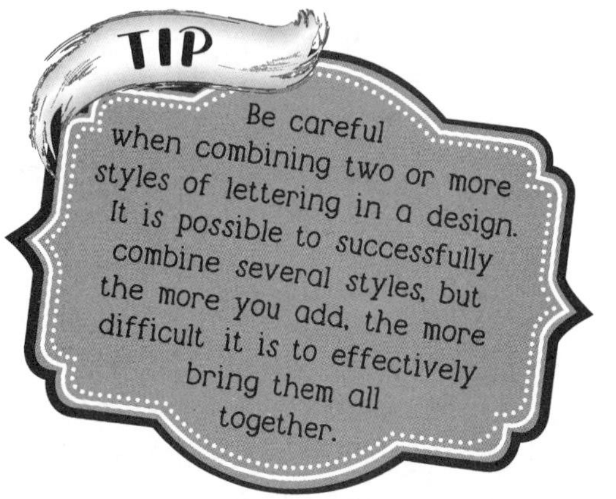

Now try to cook up your own spicily sweet design!

Think Big!

Learning to draw script within a circle will really take your lettering skills to the next level! This design looks tricky and impressive, but with these simple rules you'll find it a piece of cake.

1. Start by drawing the inner circle's guidelines so you make sure you don't run out of room. Draw a descender line, mean line (the guideline for the middle of your letter) and ascender line. Repeat this process for the larger circle, just making sure that you leave a gap between the new descender line and the inner circle's ascender line. You can erase the inner circle's ascender line once you've lettered this circle, so you don't get confused. Next add regular diagonal lines from the center of the circle to help you angle your script correctly as it loops around. Next, sketch a basic single-line script within your guides. Be patient! You may have to sketch it a few times to get the spacing and letter-width right. Keep a stack of tracing paper nearby for each stage and copy each one as you go. That way you can go back a step or two if necessary. When you are happy, add flourishes off the letters to make it look special.

2. Start adding thicks and thins to the script. This design is quite complicated but it should feel light, so try to keep your thicks from becoming too heavy. Make sure that the ends of the ascenders and descenders are squared off nicely for easier reading. Add thicks and thins to the flourishes, too!

3. Phew! That was a lot of work. Now that you have finalized your beautiful circle design, grab a good pen or marker to ink in your sketch. If you've done a lot of erasing on your piece, use the tracing paper to transfer the lines and then create a new final artwork on a new piece of paper and ink in your design!

Brush- and Calligraphy- Style Flourishes

Adding decorative flourishes to your lettering makes it stand out. Practicing loops and swirls will help develop your own style. Here are a few flourishes to get you started; trace over the gray outlines and repeat them a few times. Then practice creating your own loops and swirls!

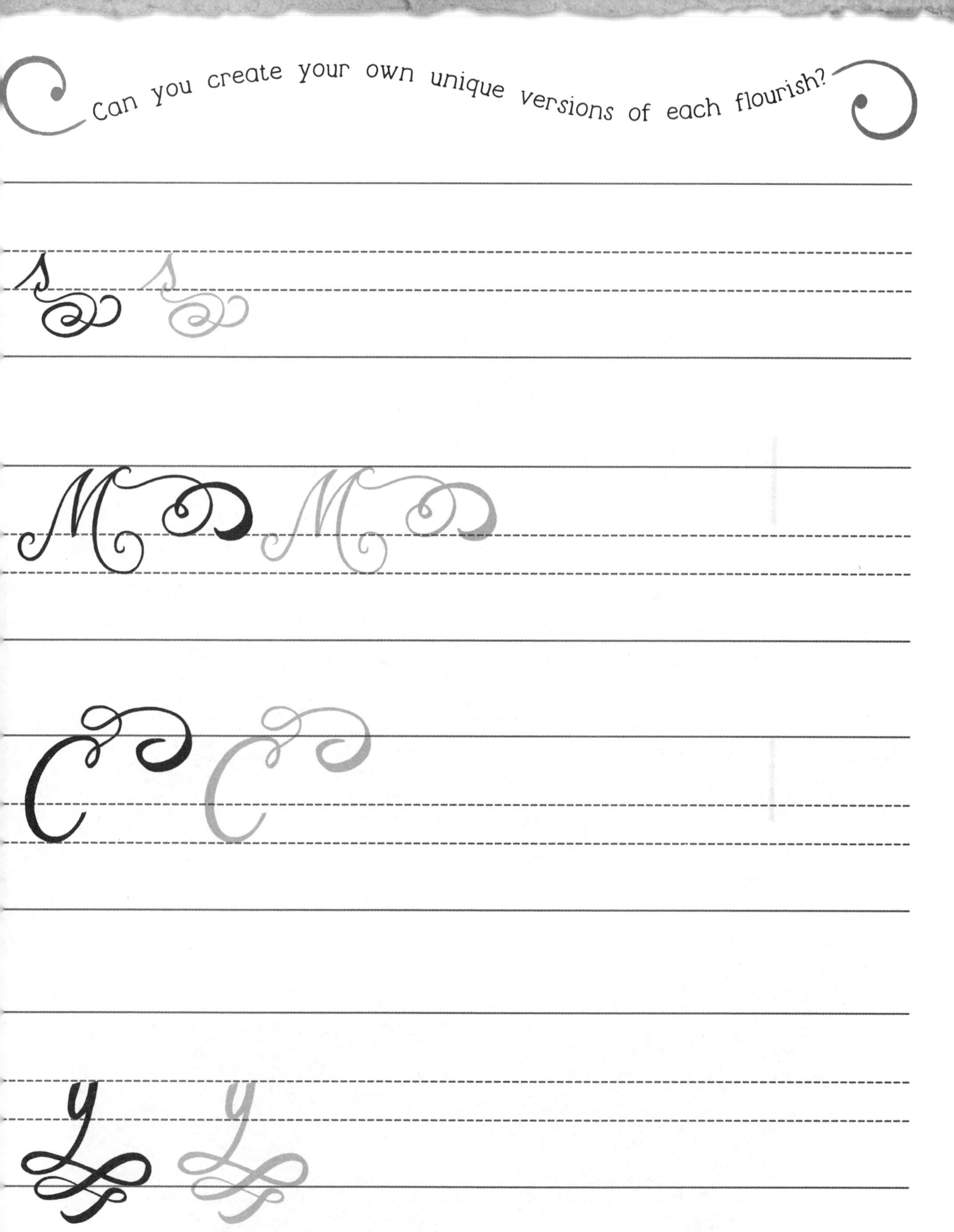
Can you create your own unique versions of each flourish?

Project Inspiration

Play with ways of connecting your letters with decorative ligatures (the extended-line flourishes used to connect two or more letters, such as those between the two t's in "Creativity").

Remember, there are no strict rules for lettering. The key thing to keep in mind is that the script should be easy to read, consistent, and fun!

Creativity
HAS NO
Rules!

Silver Screen

Lights, pencils, action! Prepare for your paper close-up as you master movie-themed lettering. The term "silver screen" came about because early-20th-century movie screens were covered in reflective silver paint, and by the late 1920s this expression was synonymous with the magic of the movies. We can bring this cinematic fun and allure to our hand-lettering through the evocative scripts commonly seen on movie posters throughout Hollywood history. There are many film genres, but some of the most imaginative lettering can be found in the styles of Western, fantasy, and horror.

Western

This style of lettering originated in the American Wild West and is commonly seen on "Wanted" posters, playbills, and casino signs. It is instantly recognizable and typically characterized by solid line work and heavy slab serifs. Western-style lettering can also be highly ornamental, with lots of flourishes and detail, much like the spurs and cowboy hats that are so familiar to fans of Westerns.

Fantasy

Fantasy-styled lettering has a rich history dating back to manuscripts of the Middle Ages (some similarities can be seen with Blackletter lettering). Although this style is wide-ranging, most fantasy lettering takes inspiration from calligraphic and other highly ornamental styles, such as the illuminated lettering of medieval monks, who used their imagination to draw fantastic creatures of myth and legend. This beautiful, whimsical style can be very elaborate with decorative flourishes and details, or it can be effectively simple with its letterforms. A common fairy-tale-style script combines a detailed drop cap with simpler lettering: perfect for adding a romantic flavor to your designs!

Horror

The only thing more surprising than this genre is its broad range of lettering styles! Horror-style scripts came into the spotlight by being featured on so many evocative movie posters. These scripts take a highly stylistic approach that very expressively reflects the eerie tone of horror movies. Sharp lines, mutated and uneven letterforms, effects like dripping blood, and gritty textures are just a few of the characteristics of this ominous style. When done well, horror-inspired lettering can stir up our emotions and have a dramatic impact!

With these main themes, plus even more out-of-this-world lettering waiting in the wings, let's draw back the curtain and begin!

Here is a full Western alphabet that you can copy or trace.
There is space provided on the opposite page to practice.

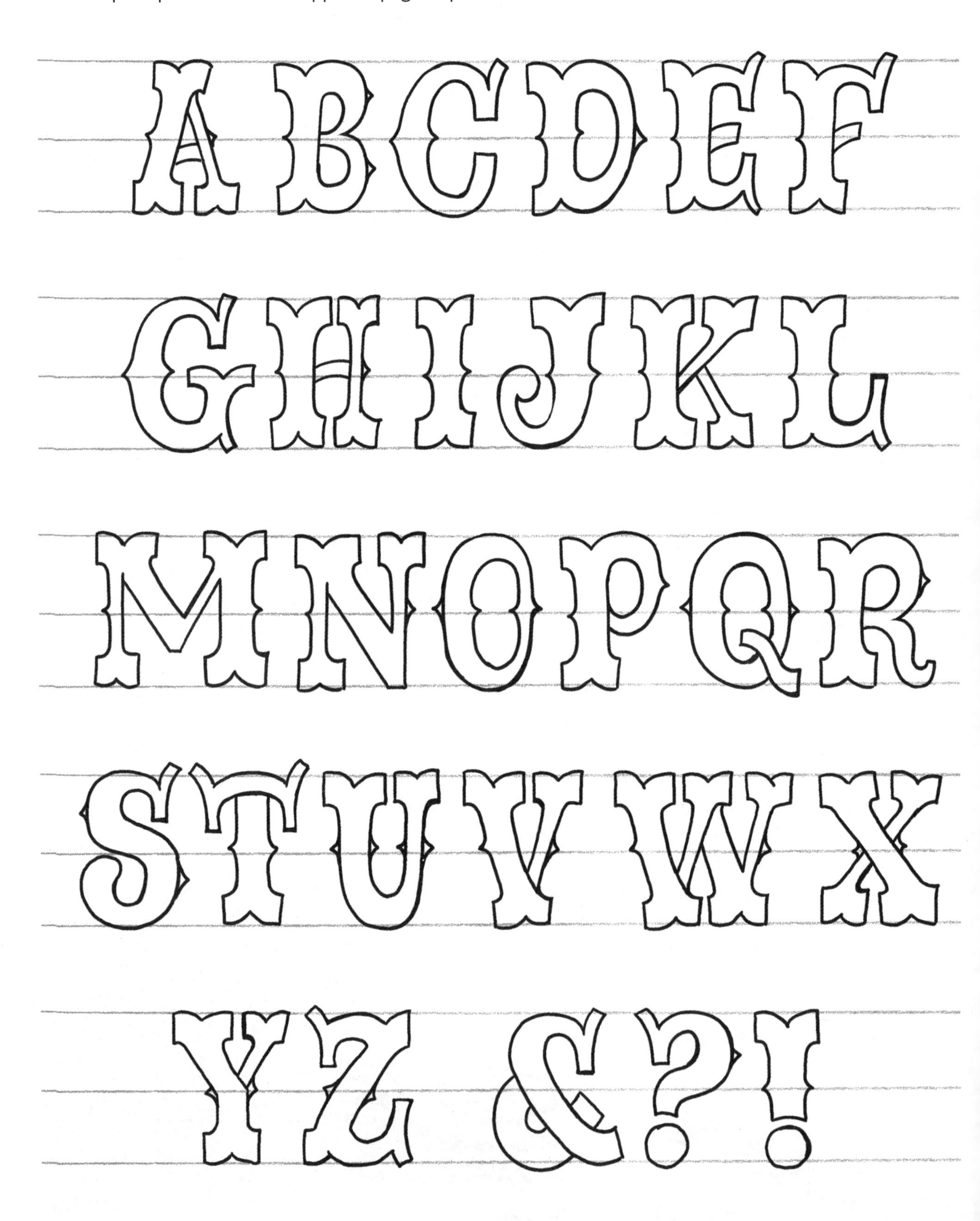

BOOTS, CHAPS, AND COWBOY HATS

Enjoy a Western state of mind! It's not just the words but also the style and mood of the lettering that takes you out to the American West. This script makes you think of small towns and wide open plains!

1. Creating a grid makes it easier to plan your composition, so first sketch out a frame for your cowboy piece. While this composition is not so formal as to require extensive guidelines, it's a good idea to map out your descender lines so that you can plan out the angles of your lettering and make sure you leave enough space for each word.

2. Start by sketching out the letter skeletons on the guidelines. Make some words larger than others; for instance, you can make key words bigger to show their greater importance. This is known as establishing a hierarchy. Add some flourishes. Once you are happy with your design, erase the grid.

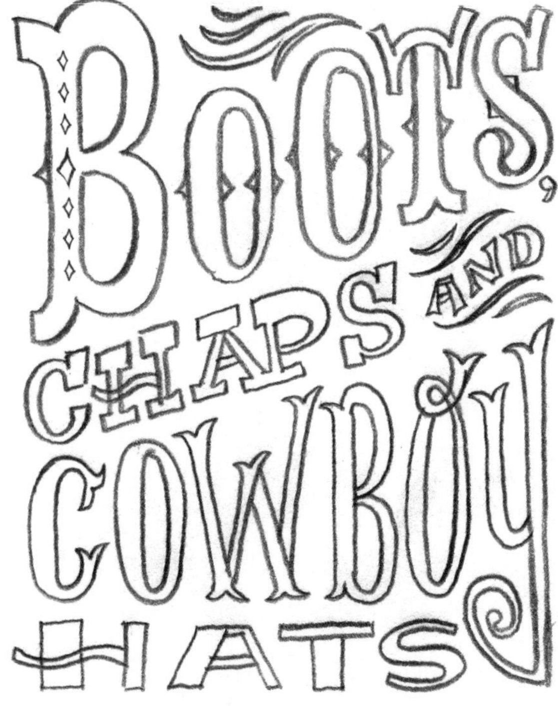

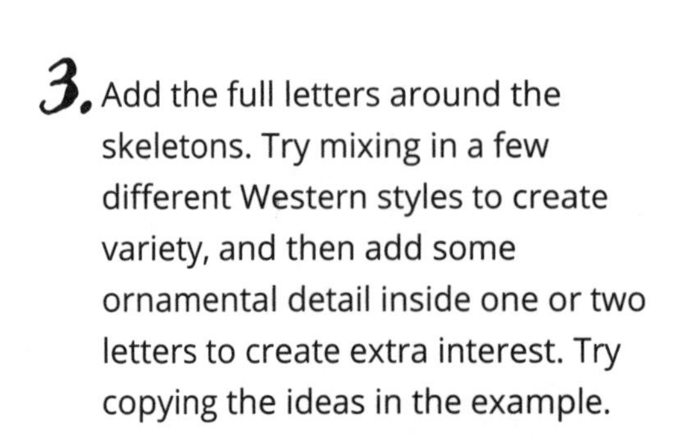

3. Add the full letters around the skeletons. Try mixing in a few different Western styles to create variety, and then add some ornamental detail inside one or two letters to create extra interest. Try copying the ideas in the example.

BOOTS, CHAPS AND COWBOY HATS

4. Now's a good time to add drop shadows behind the letters of any words you would like to emphasize. When drawing a drop shadow you need to imagine a light is shining on to the letters and creating a shadow behind them (in this case the light is in the upper-right and is casting a shadow to the lower-right of the lettering). Draw a faint line going around the letters on the opposite side to this light source, solidifying the letters' shadows.

Then, to finish your drawing, use a pen or marker to ink over your sketch. You can vary the color and tone of different words. You can see here how using a lighter color for "CHAPS" and "HATS" adds some interesting contrast. Finally, erase any pencil marks when it's dry. Alternatively, if there are still sketch marks visible, you can copy this lettering onto tracing paper. You can copy any of the projects in this way if you want to transfer them to a fresh piece of paper or save them as a template for future use.

This Western-style lettering is designed to clearly convey information with a punch! You're the lettering-sheriff in town: try it out for yourself!

1. Begin by sketching a grid for your letters. Here we've divided the space into the five sections that we need for this piece. As you add each section, very lightly sketch in a test letter from each word in that section. This helps to make sure there's enough room for you to hand-letter in and that the letters look good at that size.

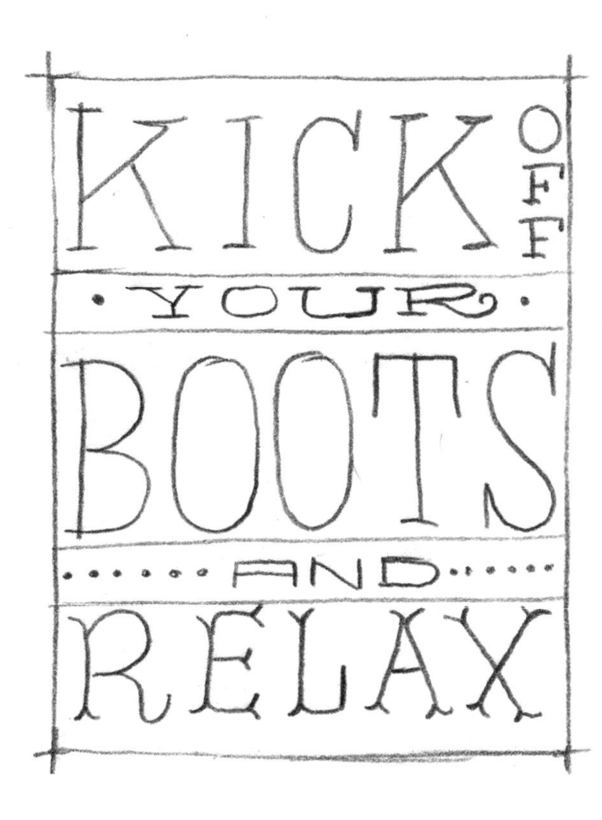

2. Using letter skeletons, fill in the grid. You can see that the main words in the phrase are the biggest in the piece. Try adding some decorations, like dots, to the gaps in between.

3. Using a few different Western styles of lettering for variety, draw in the letters. This example includes the lettering script from the Western alphabet and also a more rounded style for "BOOTS" and the smaller words. Having some lettering without decoration can also stop your composition from looking overwhelming: here, "OFF," "YOUR," and "AND" are all quite plain. Add some serifs to "YOUR," and a plaque-like frame around it. Finally, add a top and bottom border with some fine-line decoration to contain your composition.

4. If you'd like to add a bit more excitement to the artwork, sketch extra details inside the letters to balance everything out. Then, using pens or markers, ink over the letters and decorations with the suggested light and dark contrasts as shown to finish your drawing, and erase any remaining pencil marks.

Try this one out for yourself, then put your feet up and chill out!

Here is a full Fairy Tale alphabet that you can copy or trace.
There is space provided on the opposite page to practice.

DREAMS DO COME TRUE

The Fairy Tale style is whimsical and enchanting, leading you into a world of fantasy, mystery, and magic. Get the style right and your audience is halfway to this dreamy feeling, even before they read the words! This project adds some simple illustrative elements and word effects to enhance this mood.

1. Sketch out a template of two sets of horizontal guidelines for the lettering. Add plain skeleton letters within the guides.

2. Draw the letterforms around the skeleton letters, using the Fairy Tale alphabet as a guide. To decorate, add some flamboyant flourishes around the words that we'll turn into vines, like those you might see climbing up a magic castle or entwined through an enchanted forest.

3. Thicken the vine flourishes and then sketch in some leaves and pretty flowers sprinkled across the composition to add a little more beauty and help balance everything out.

4. To complete your drawing, use a pen or marker to ink over your sketch and erase any pencil marks. If the artwork needs a bit more detailing, add some art to the inside of each letter. Be consistent with your decoration for each word: you could put white dots (using a white pen) on one word and linework on another, for instance, but don't do both on the same word.

Now it's your turn to create a happy ending for this lettering activity!

Fairy-tale styles of script can be ornate or simple, but are always fun. See how many different styles of the same word you can come up with! This exercise is one of the best ways to become confident within a lettering genre; learning various sub-styles will also increase the breadth of your lettering skills. Look for opportunities to have fun with the ascenders, descenders, and ornate details to give each composition a different personality.

What other fantasy fairy-tale styles can you magic up?
FAIRY TALE
FAIRY TALE
FAIRY TALE
FAIRY TALE

THROUGH the WOODS

This time we are looking to create a fantasy forest theme with our letters. For this script, we draw sticks and branches to make up the words, and then scatter them with leaves and flowers. This can be great for elfin-like fantasy themes.

1. For this phrase think of Little Red Riding Hood! It is perfect for using a fantasy forest theme. Lightly sketch out the letter skeletons for your stiff, wood-like lettering and mix in some script lettering too.

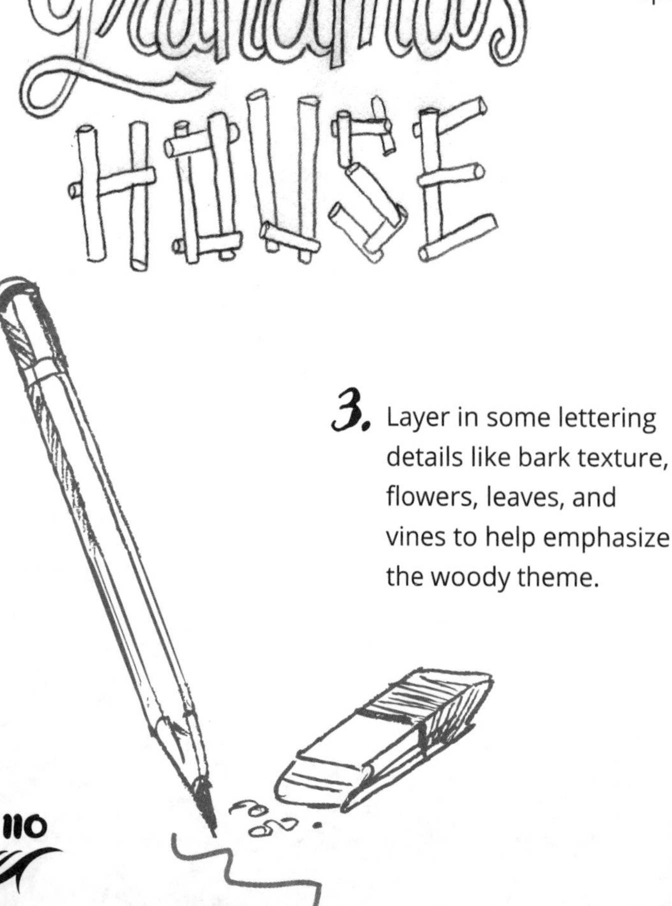

2. Draw the rest of your letter shape around the skeletons. Overlap the wood lettering in places (as if you were actually fitting pieces of physical wood together), and include a few twigs sprouting out of the branches for variety.

3. Layer in some lettering details like bark texture, flowers, leaves, and vines to help emphasize the woody theme.

4. Finalize your drawing by using pens or markers to ink over your sketch with the suggested lighter and darker contrasts illustrated here, and then erase any pencil marks. If you think the design could do with some technicolor, try adding some bright splashes of color onto the flowers, leaves, and bark!

Now, venture into the woods and try this one yourself!

Rise of the Zombies

This fantastically fun horror-style script will really stretch your creativity. Try it out and thrill your friends with your awesome skills!

1. Sketch out two arched rectangles as guides. Lightly add your letter skeletons. Try stacking the less important words on top of each other to shake up the composition.

2. Draw letterforms around the plain letter skeletons. Use a brush-stroke-inspired style for the top row of letters with a sharp, scratchy edge for the terminals. Use a shaky but bold styling for "ZOMBIES" and add slime-like drips.

3. Fill in the words on the top row and add a drop shadow to the bottom word. To further emphasize "ZOMBIES," add some detailing to the insides of the letters.

4. To finalize your drawing, use pens or markers to ink over your sketch. Use a lighter tone or color to fill in "ZOMBIES"—try adding an eerie color, perhaps a ghoulish green? Don't forget to use a contrasting color, in this case a darker one, for the drop shadow to make sure it stands apart from the main lettering.

Now it's your turn to use your braaaains and create some awesome lettering!

Let's Get Creative!

Be daring! Sometimes it's good to break away from a traditional lettering grid. Choose a horror-themed phrase and try drawing a simple silhouette shape to match—something like a pumpkin, a tombstone, or a witch's hat. Make sure it's big enough to fit the phrase in! Try to create your lettering like a puzzle, with descenders and ascenders that fit together inside the shape and fill the space nicely. Make some words larger and use a variety of spooky lettering styles. When you have finalized your lettering, ink it in and then fill in the rest of the shape so the letters stand out.

BE A MAD SCIENTIST AND SEE WHAT SHAPES, SHADOWS, AND SILHOUETTES YOU CAN CREATE FOR YOUR LETTERS!

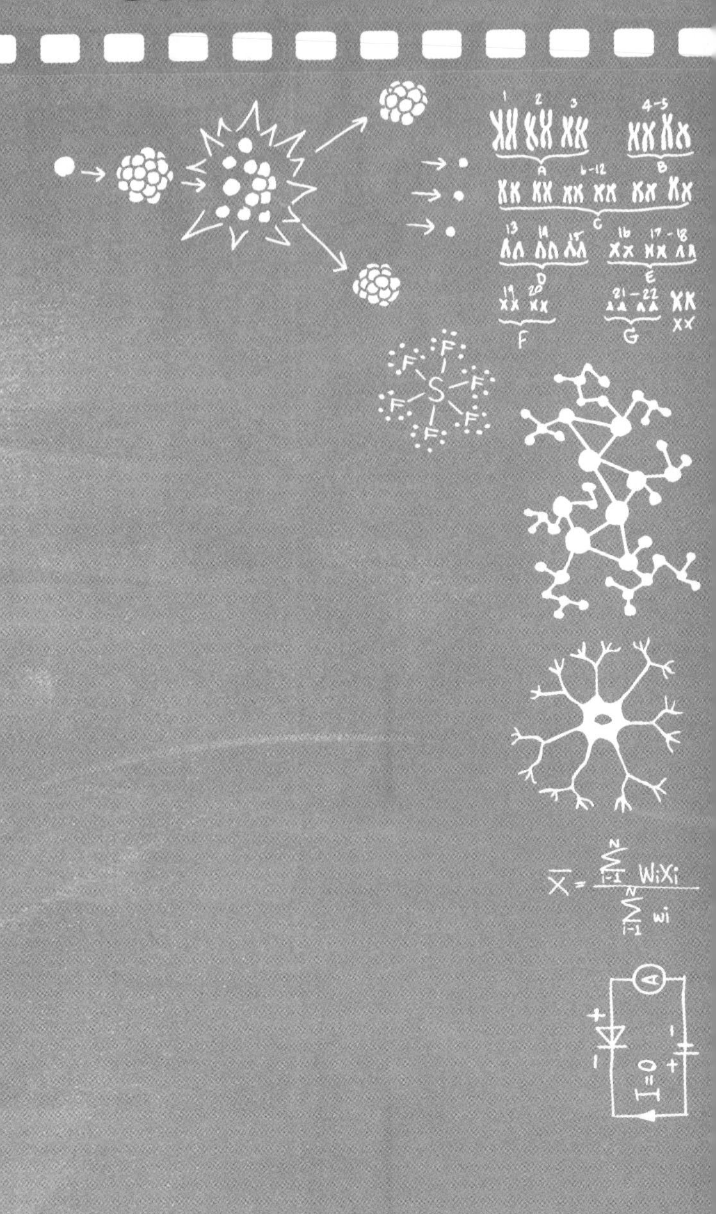

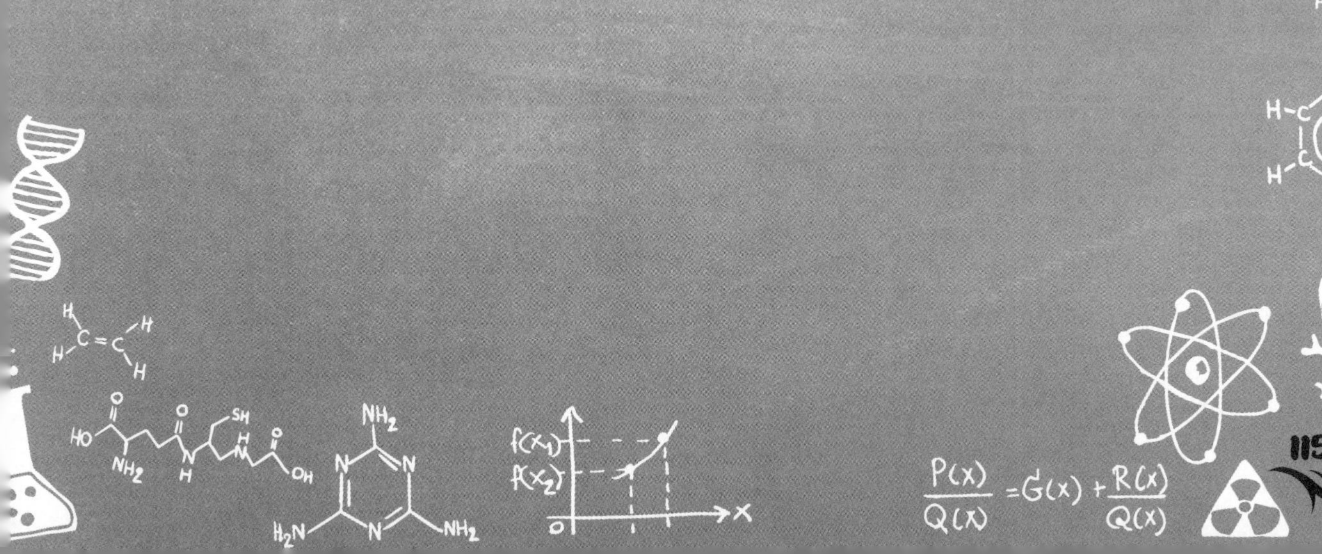

ATTACK OF THE GIANT LETTERS

Lights, camera, action movie! For this project, the towering letters and their special effects plunge you straight into the excitement of an adventure movie! The 3-D letters loom out at you; they are also decorated to look like they are ruins within a wild jungle.

1. This is an exercise in creating extruded lettering (lettering that looks 3-D or as though it is sticking out). Sketch two arched rectangles as guides, then lightly sketch the letter skeletons inside them. Use capitals to make it look momentous! Stack some of the less important words to add interest to the composition.

2. Create the rest of the letterforms around the skeletons. For the larger words, try a shakier style to emulate jagged rocks.

3. Add an adventurous atmosphere to the main words by sketching cracks and vines on each letter. Now for the really spectacular part! Draw a giant drop shadow that follows the shape of each of the letters, increasingly slanting it dramatically to the right. Make sure that the thickness of the shadows matches the thickness of the strokes that make up each letter. This will create an awesome 3-D effect!

4. Finalize your drawing with a pen or marker to ink over your sketch. By filling in the counters (holes) in your letters and shading in the shadow behind the words, the letters will really look like they are extruding out of the page.

TIP

When creating 3-D letters it's easier to practice with a single letter first until you get more confident. The easiest letters to start with are the ones with straight edges, like I, H, and T. Letters with curved edges like O are much harder.

Get cracking and have a giant go at creating this project!

SPACE

Create stellar science-fiction-style lettering by angling and shading your letters so that they appear to be 3-D and floating freely in space! Vary the angle of each letter so that they all face in a slightly different direction, then add stars to emphasize the space theme. To embellish this artwork a bit more, use pencil shading to give the letters a shiny metallic look, which creates a classic sci-fi feel.

Try your own out-of-this-world shading style here!

EXPERIMENT AND BOLDLY DISCOVER YOUR OWN UNCHARTED SCI-FI LETTERING STYLES!

Try combining the three styles of Western, fantasy, and horror into one composition! As you sketch the words, slant them to create a dynamic flow. Give each word its own lettering detail, then round out your artwork with a drop shadow to pull everything happily together!

CARTOON, COMIC, & GRAFFITI

Lettering doesn't just have to be serious and rule-bound; it can be fun, creative, and zany! Discover the alternative world of hand-lettering for comics, cartoons, and graffiti, where pretty much anything can happen! These hugely popular styles can be seen all over the place: in comic strips, in cartoons, or in street-art murals.

Cartoon

Animated cartoons were developed in the early 1900s and a matching lettering style soon followed; first in the silent era to describe the action and then later in speech bubbles. Cartoon lettering plays with shapes and the meanings of words in funny and novel ways, something that comic lettering also does. In the late 1980s, computerized digital fonts arrived. They became popular but are not as versatile as the original hand-lettering. Cartoon and comic lettering are both perfect for any sort of project where you want a fun or amusing look!

Comic

Comic lettering is much older than the familiar comics of today. The style dates back hundreds of years to when it was used inside the speech bubbles of political cartoons and advertisements. Until the 1980s, most cartoonists drew lettering directly onto the pencil-sketched pages of a comic book prior to inking! Because comics are a moving story, their lettering developed to express the narrative: for example, "speedy" could be drawn in long, stretched-out italics, while "fat" could look short and squishy. Today, most comic lettering is done digitally. But you can use that original personalized comic and cartoon lettering to give a special and original touch to birthday cards, folders, and book covers, and, of course, in comics!

GRAFFITI

Graffiti is as old as writing, with examples even found back in ancient Egypt and Rome! This originally unlawful lettering style has grown in popularity and acceptability, and has become commercialized. In New York City in the late 1960s, graffiti appeared on subway cars, bridges, buildings, walls, and industrial wastelands: in fact, pretty much everywhere! This art style became into a symbol of modern urban living. Now it's often commissioned as art for public walls and for businesses, like cafes. As an art form, graffiti is an unrestricted form of expression and appears in a variety of genre styles that are often a mystery to the uninitiated. The graffiti style contributes sheer excitement and exuberance to lettering, and a distinct lack of rules. It's a great lettering style to use if you're creating your own posters or making labels for your books.

These awesome alternative styles are bursting with fun and exciting new hand-lettering techniques—so let's get started!

BUBBLE

Here is a full cartoon-style bubble alphabet that you can copy or trace. There is space provided on the opposite page to practice.

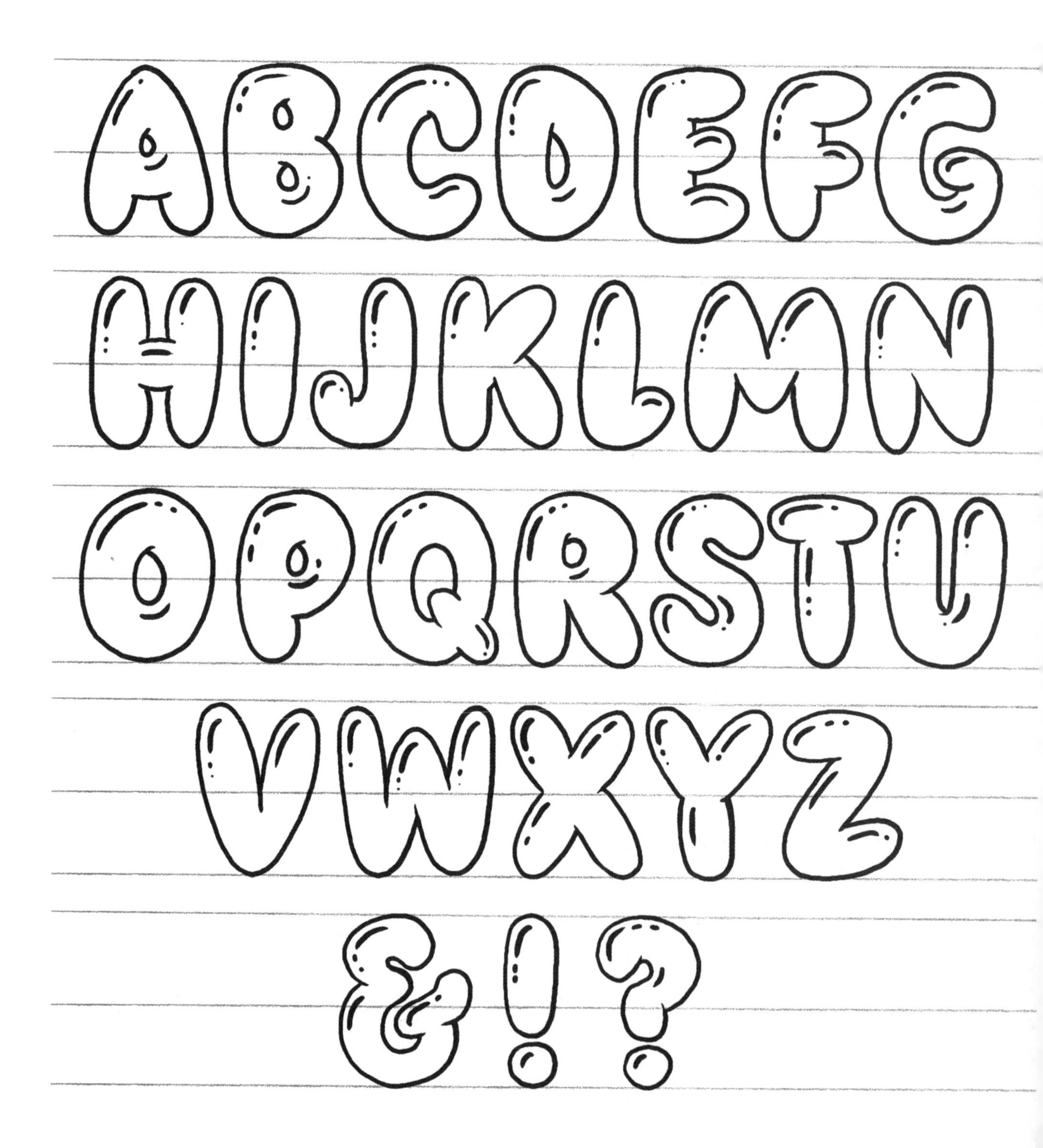

FLOAT AWAY

If the look and feel of your letters reflect the meaning of the words, they almost become a picture of your message! In true cartoon style, the lettering for "FLOAT AWAY" is drawn to resemble balloons drifting off into the air.

1. This airy project doesn't need guidelines; it has a looser structure. The letters start at two different baselines and are all at slightly different angles. This helps give the impression that the letters are floating! Lightly sketch the letter skeletons, making sure you leave enough space between each letter to then add their bulging bubble letterforms. You may need to shift letters over slightly as you go, but leave a little of each letter overlapping with its surrounding letters.

2. Erase the skeleton letters and any overlapping letter outlines, allowing some letters to come to the front and others to sit behind. This helps to create a sense of depth by making it look as if some 3-D balloons are floating in front of others.

3. Add accent lines and dots around the bulging curves of the letters, as shown in the example. This creates the effect of light reflecting off a shiny balloon surface. You can also make the letters look more like balloons by adding balloon knots and trailing strings to the letters. You don't need to do this for every letter if the bottom of that letter is covered by another.

4. Ink in your letters and erase any pencil lines when dry. Alternatively, copy them onto tracing paper (something you can do for all the projects in this section if you want to create a template or to transfer the design to another piece of paper). If you want to take your artwork to the next level, use markers or colored pencils to add dots, stripes, and shading to the balloons!

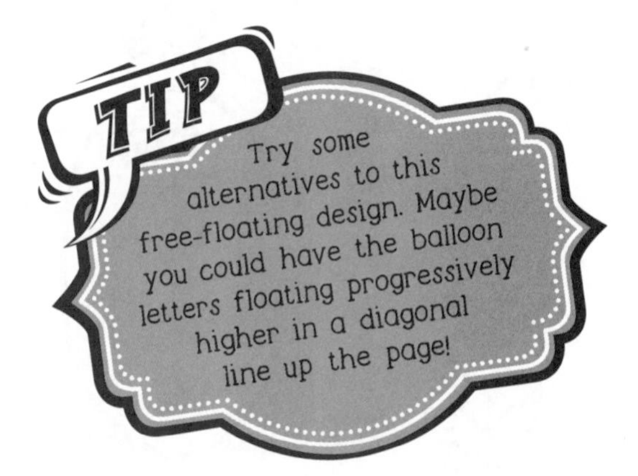

Now it's your turn to float some lettering ideas around!

LET'S GET CREATIVE!

It's great fun to draw cartoon-style phrases made up of lots of different characters and effects! How many different ideas can you come up with?

Draw your full name using as many different quirky styles as possible. Mix it up: make some letters bold and chunky and others thin, some curled and others straight. Add patterns or stripes to some and fill in others. You can even turn a letter into a character that suits its shape: for example, make O into a smiley face and Y into an open-mouthed sea monster! The key is making every letter different. Use the opposite page to have fun and play around with different ideas!

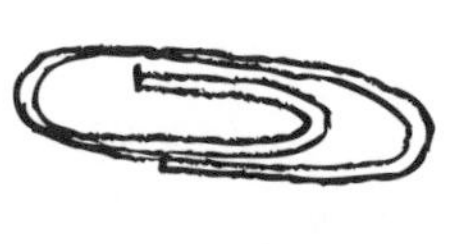

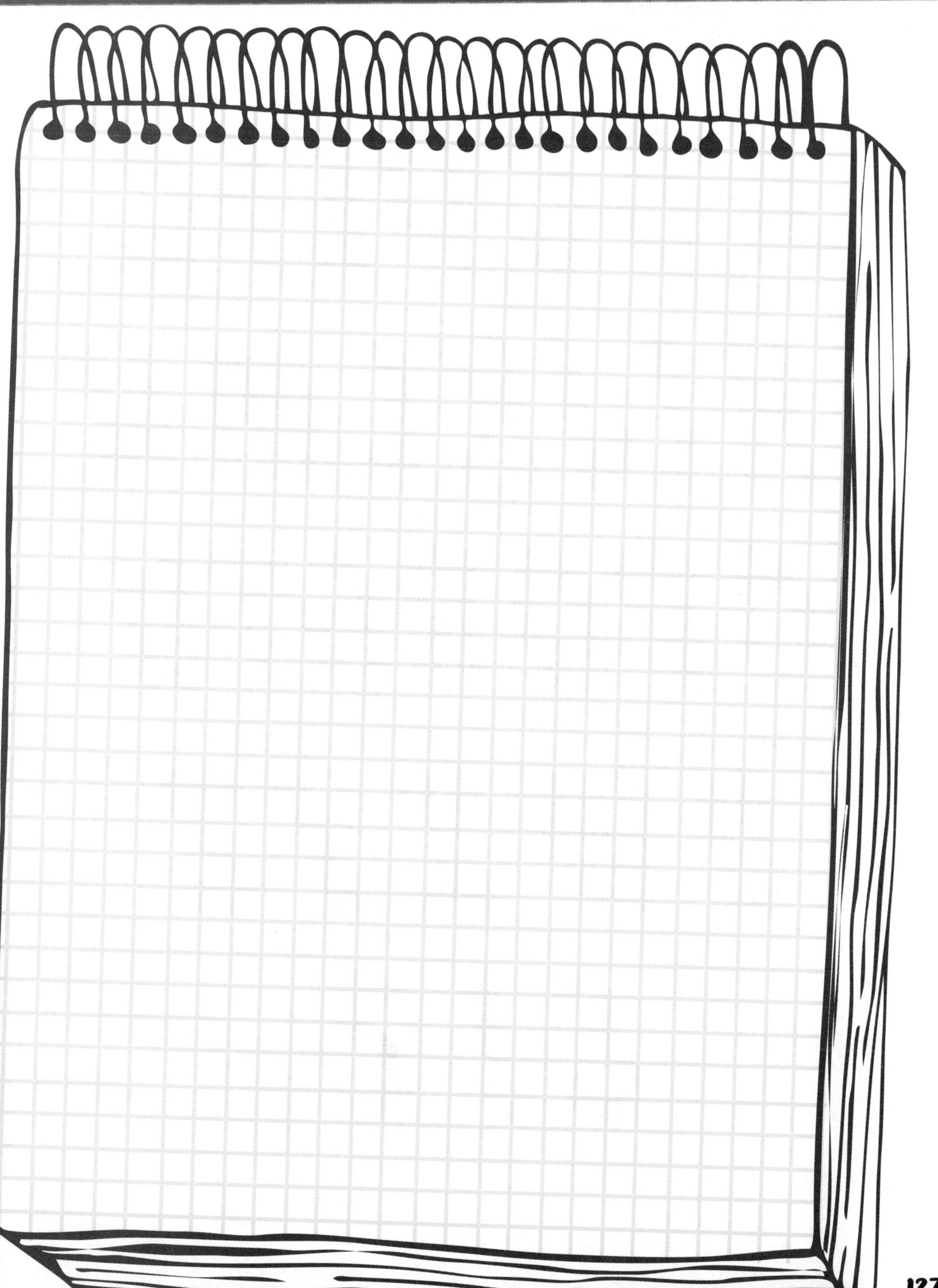

Here is a full comic-style alphabet that you can copy or trace.
There is space provided on the opposite page to practice.

ABCDEFG

HIJKLMN

OPQRSTU

VWXYZ

&!?

ULTRA AVENGER

Not all comics are based around funny cartoons: many tell exciting adventure stories, which can variously include superheroes, detectives, or spaceships battling across the galaxy. These comics have a completely different mood to a humorous comic and so require a stronger, more forceful style of lettering.

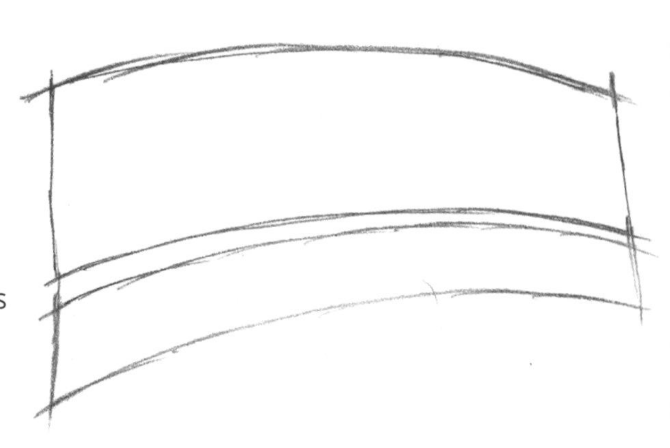

1. Lightly sketch two slightly arched, skewed rectangles as guides to fit your lettering inside.

2. Start by drawing your letter skeletons, and then form each superhero-style letter around them. Notice how this lettering style is a bold, which means it is heavy looking with thick letter-widths. Remember to stay within your frame guidelines and ensure the lettering stands up straight. Once you are happy with your work, carefully erase the letter skeletons.

3. You can now make the block letters look 3-D, which will add a further sense of bulk and overall impact to the composition. Draw diagonal lines and sides to all the letters, making sure you use the same angle for each so that the depth is consistent. You can also sketch in another curved rectangular line parallel to "ULTRA" and above "AVENGER" to help you keep the letters the same size.

4. To make "ULTRA" stand out more, add an inline (a line of contrasting color to the main letter outline that runs around the inside edge of a letter). Color in or shade the three-dimensional sides of the letters, leaving the top area white for variation. Adding stylized stripes for the shading on the sides of "ULTRA" creates a cool superhero-styled look!

5. Using pens or markers, ink over your sketch with the suggested shading contrasts below to finalize your drawing, then erase any pencil marks when dry. To make the artwork pop even more, add some color to the words, using a light shade so that it still reads clearly. Maybe choose the costume colors of your favorite superhero!

TIP

Don't forget to make your counters (the holes in letters such as A and R) in block style or to shade them when making them 3-D. Otherwise your composition will look off.

Up, up, and away, superheroes! Let's get lettering!

Sounds and Bursts

One of the most fun parts of comic lettering is creating novelty lettering that uses flourishes to convey the meaning or mood of the words themselves. Let's explore and practice some fun comic effects.

Adding Special Effects

You can add drips under, around, and inside your lettering to add interest. Don't go too crazy though: adding too many drips can get very messy. Less is more!

Creating Depth

Add emphasis to your lettering by creating some depth around the letters: it looks great with basically every style! Play around with the direction of the shadow and with how exaggerated the shadow is (how deep it extends or how dark it is) to see what different looks you can create. Adding depth to the bubble lettering, for instance, makes it look more inflated and friendly!

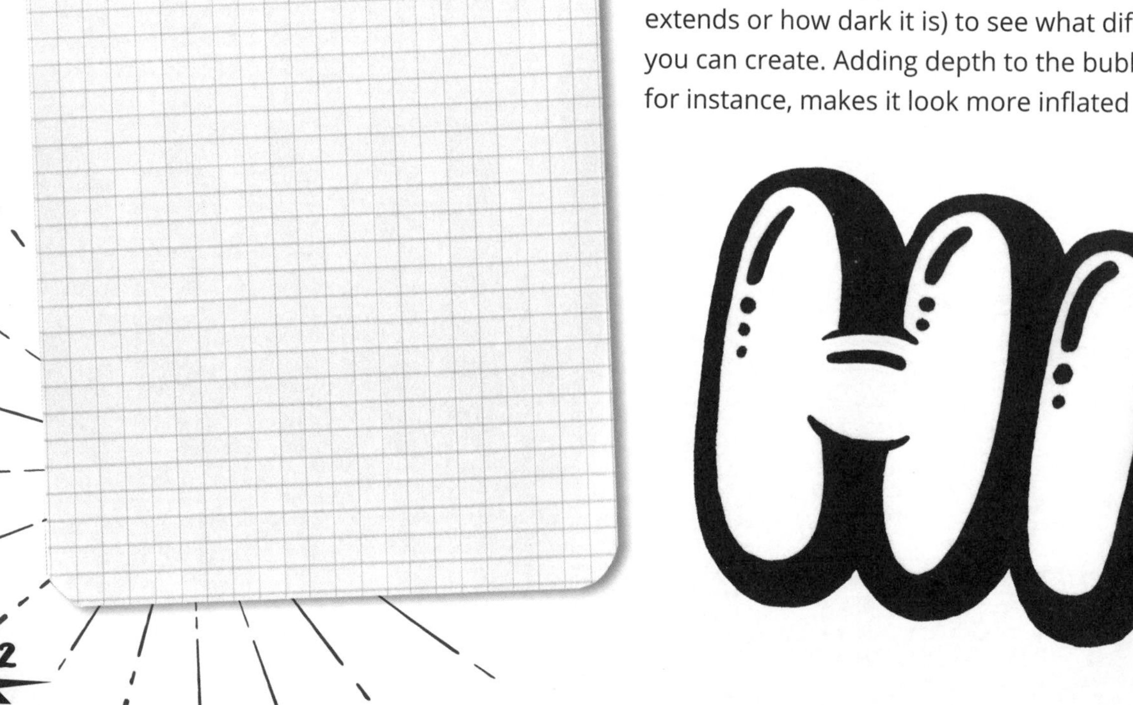

Motion Blur Lines

Motion blur lines are a great way to give the illusion of movement to your lettering. Decide which direction you want your letterforms to move, then add some motion lines behind them in the opposite direction. This is a great way to suggest a superhero moving very fast!

Radiating Shapes

If you want to accentuate a word, try adding some shapes or lines radiating out around it, like these lightning bolts. To push it even further, add a shape behind the artwork as well, like this pointy sound bubble. This all works to suggest the crackle, energy, and electricity of a superhero laser blast!

COMIC EFFECTS

Sound effects are staples of cartoon and comic scripts! Their importance is often overlooked, but they offer letterers a great opportunity to get creative with expression and are super fun to add to your drawings and designs.

1. Lightly draw a skewed rectangle with a slight arc as a guide for your lettering. Sketch the phrase "AHHHH!" as a skeleton frame, leaving adequate space between each letter. When you're happy with the composition, add bold letterforms around your frame.

2. Erase the letter skeletons, any overlapping lines, and the arced rectangular guide. Add dimension to the letters by sketching in their sides and tops, making sure you to use the same perspective throughout.

3. Finalize your drawing by inking over your sketch with a pen or marker and erasing any pencil lines once it dries.

Now it's your turn to make some lettering noise!

Think about the sounds that words make and try to capture that sound in your lettering style. These sorts of words are called *onomatopoeic* words.
Try lettering some of these words in the shapes below.
Use the examples for inspiration.

GRAFITTI

Here is a full graffiti-style alphabet that you can copy or trace.
There is space provided on the opposite page to practice.

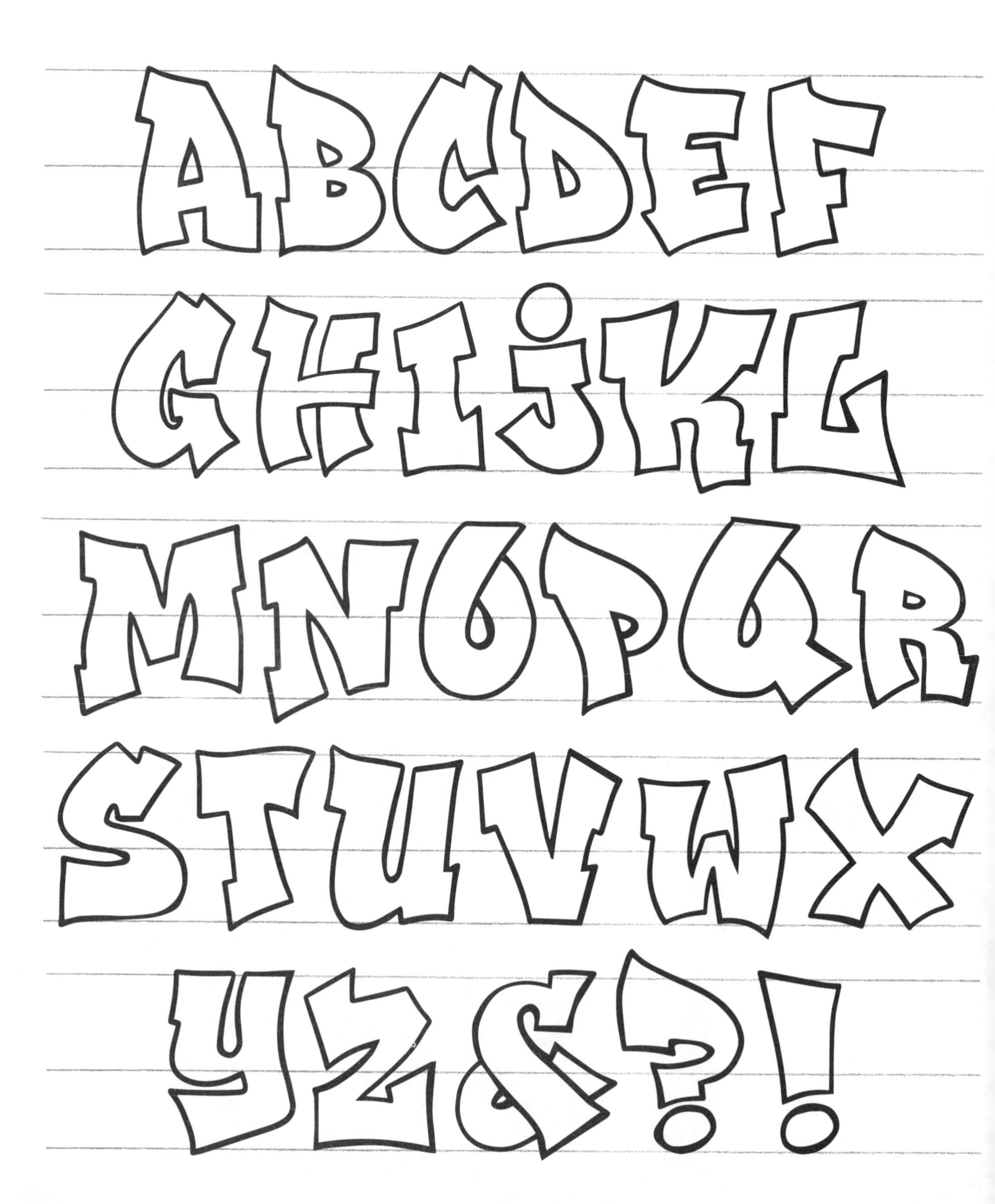

FRESH

Graffiti script is a fun, wild, totally expressive style of lettering. It's ideal for creating an exciting statement message to display!

1. Lightly sketch out your lettering skeleton, then start to build up each graffiti letterform around it. Overlap each character, as this creates a dynamic look.

2. Erase the letter skeletons and any bottom-layer overlapping lines. To help give the letters the appearance of depth, add a shadow (known as a drop shadow) behind them then color or shade it in.

3. Add a stroke outline around the entire word following the contour of each character. Layer in more effects, like a speckled pattern inside the letters. Start the shading at the bottom of the letterforms and gradually fade it out as you move up to the top.

4. Finalize your drawing by inking over your sketch with pens or markers, paying attention to the different shades of contrast that you can see. Then erase any remaining pencil lines after the ink has dried. Use markers or colored pencils to layer in more depth by coloring in the outer stroke. You can always transfer this design and scale it up on a poster page to stick on your bedroom wall.

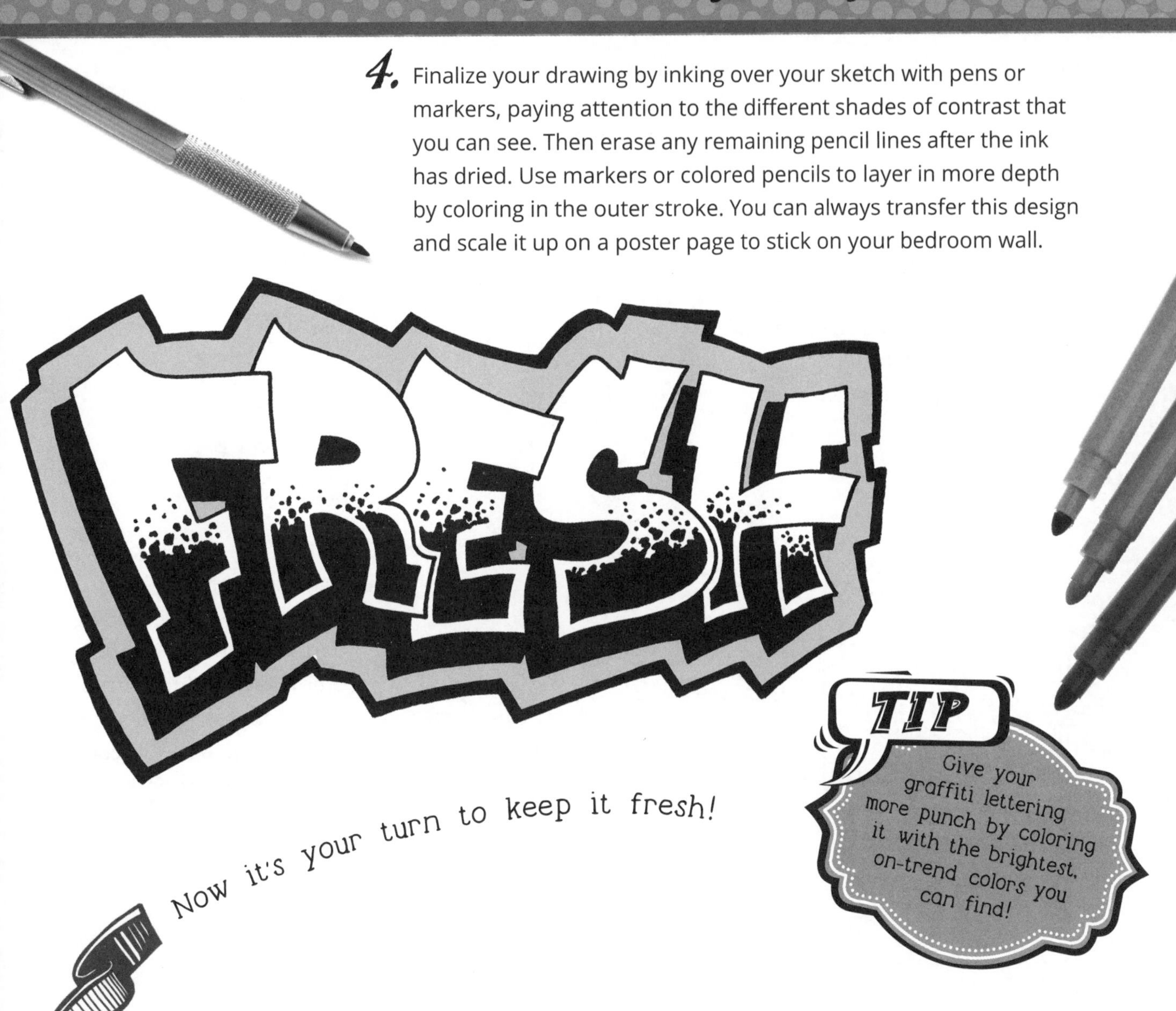

TIP

Give your graffiti lettering more punch by coloring it with the brightest, on-trend colors you can find!

Now it's your turn to keep it fresh!

FREESTYLE

In this project, the letters dance around each other in an almost three-dimensional way. It may look a little daunting, but follow each stage carefully and you'll soon succeed.

1. Lightly sketch your letter skeletons, overlapping some of the letters. Add arrows and accents around the letters to add interest and movement.

2. Add some thin blocks around the letter skeletons, including the arrow flourishes on some of the terminals and the surrounding decorations. For the overlapping letters, it looks extra cool if you make them interlock, like you can see with the T overlapping like a hook over the Y's ascender.

3. Erase the skeletons inside each character, then add a three-dimensional drop-shadow shape behind each of the letterforms. This can get a bit confusing, so sketch lightly and try to maintain the same angle throughout.

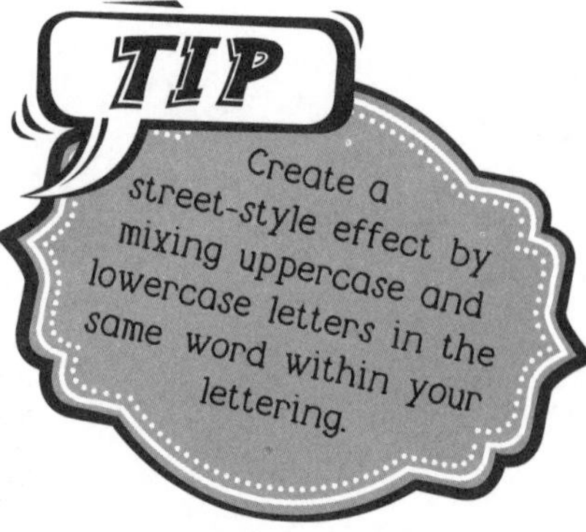

4. Ink over your sketch with pens or markers, then erase any pencil marks when dry. Alternatively, copy it onto tracing paper. Color in the drop shadow in a darker shade and try adding a shape behind the lettering. In this case there is a computer-graphic-like pixel effect. Use markers or pencils to add a pop of color!

Break the rules and create your own graffiti-style lettering!

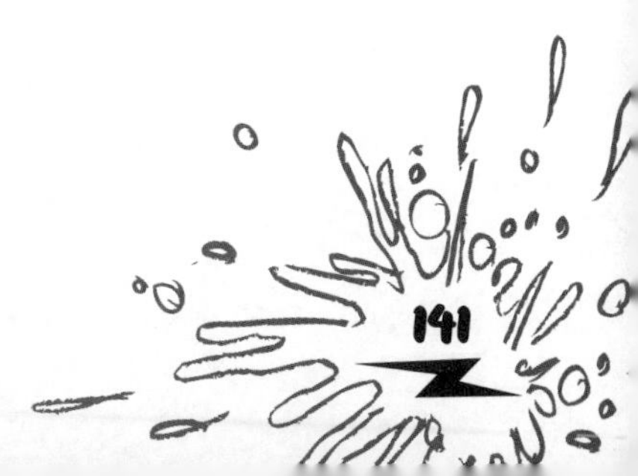

Let's Get Creative!

A great warm-up exercise is to practice single letters in as many styles as possible: think drop shadows, highlights, shading, curves, rotating letters at different angles, and more! This will make you a more versatile letterer and your work will look more exciting too! Check out these examples, then have a go and see what you can create for comic-, graffiti-, and cartoon-style letters.

H A P M O Y N W B D R

FREEDOM
IS A
BLANK PIECE
OF PAPER

PROJECT INSPIRATION

Mix up multiple lettering styles of differing weights into one composition to create a dynamic and bold statement. This piece uses some of the comic, graffiti, and cartoon lettering styles as inspiration. Map out a grid and lightly sketch out the phrase before you begin. Try to balance the composition and emphasize any important words. Then take a chance and give it a go!

CHALK BOARD techniques

JESSICA MATTHEWS

CHALKBOARD TECHNIQUES

CHALKBOARD Techniques

Chalk lettering is super fun and super simple! Here are lots of step-by-step examples and photos of this very distinct hand-lettering medium to inspire and guide you. What could be easier, cheaper, and more satisfying artistically? Have a go and find out for yourself!

What is chalk lettering?

Chalkboard lettering can look daunting but it's actually deceptively easy! The processes you'll learn in this chapter will teach you the basics and build up your confidence, so you will soon be able to create amazing works of art on your own. Don't be disheartened if at first it doesn't look "perfect" —the best thing about chalk lettering is that it is supposed to look individual and hand-done, so any little differences you introduce just enhance these qualities. At any rate, you'll get better with each board that you create. Plus, if you make a mistake you can just rub it out and start again!

This chapter shows you how to create beautiful pieces of chalkboard art that can be practical—(like signs or reminders)—but above all, brighten up your space! The most important tip for great chalk lettering is to have fun and let your personality shine through. Aim to make each piece individual and unique, and you'll feel like a pro in no time!

What is chalk lettering used for?

Because it's such a simple, fun, and economical do-it-yourself (DIY) craft, chalkboard lettering has become really on trend in recent times. Much of this is thanks to popular design-based websites, where people can create and highlight works of art then showcase them to other DIYers around the world. Going online is a great place to check out other chalk-letterers and design trends for inspiration!

Keep an eye out for chalk lettering being used for event signage, and for menus and special boards in cafés and restaurants. It can also be used around the home—think of beautifully decorated notice-boards or planners. You can use chalk lettering outside for event signage or photo walls, or paint signs for your bedroom and chalk up messages and notices. The chalk lettering possibilities are endless, but some of the greatest ideas are explored in this section!

Materials

You only need a few items to get started:

- Chalk (white and/or colored)
- Two-hole pencil sharpener (the big hole is used to give the chalk a sharp and accurate tip for your lettering)
- Chalk pens (variously colored). These are also referred to as "chalk markers" and are used for more permanent designs. Chalk pens can usually be removed using a wet cloth, but it can take some serious effort to remove the residue!
- Cloths (both wet and dry)
- Cotton tips (for erasing fine detail)
- Pencil
- Paper
- Ruler
- Eraser
- Chalk duster

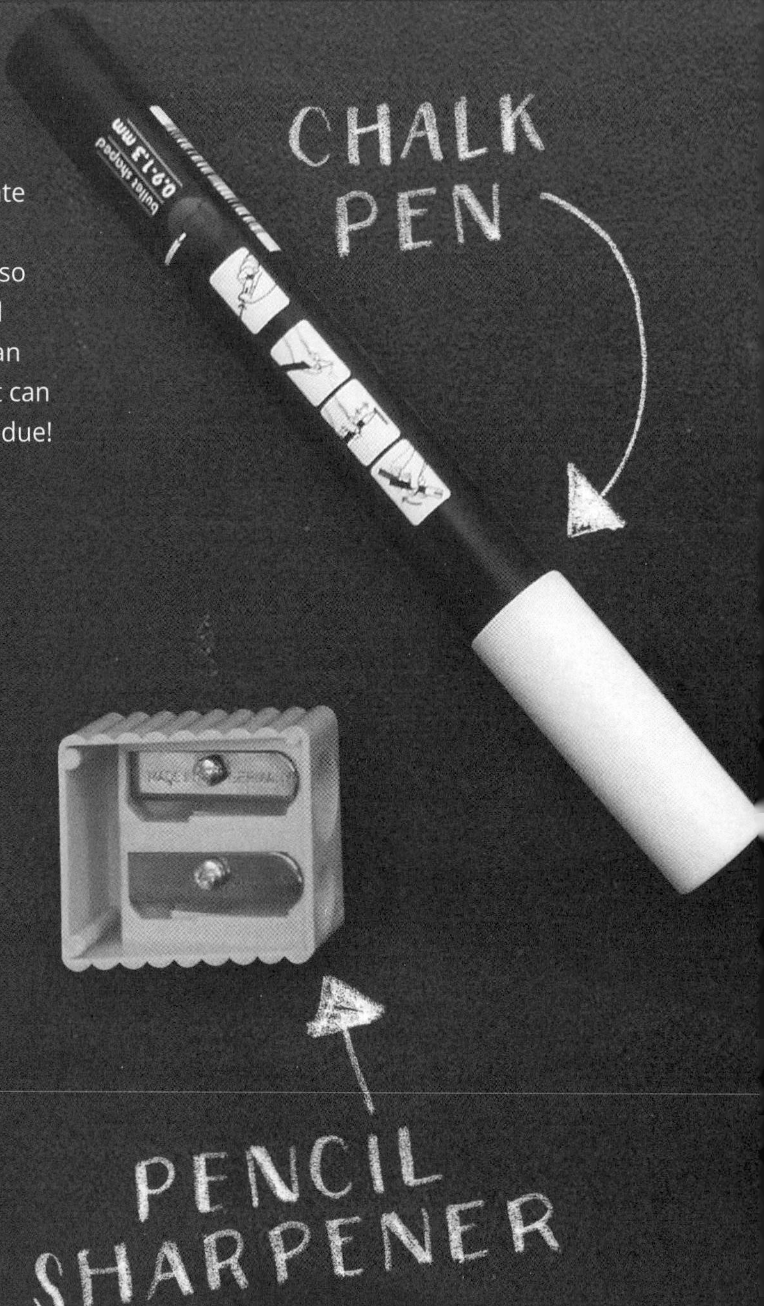

CHALK PEN

Get ready for a lot of chalk dust!

PENCIL SHARPENER

CHALK DUSTER

RULER

CHALK

ERASER

COTTON TIPS

CLOTH

COLORED CHALK

PENCIL

Start by "seasoning" your board. This prevents "ghosting," which is when you've erased your mistake but a faint line still remains. Seasoning is best done outside as it will create a lot of dust. However, it isn't essential to season your board if you prefer the true black of the board as contrast.

To season a chalkboard: find a hard surface—such as an outside wall—and evenly rub a full piece of chalk across it to remove the chalk's shiny protective coating. Then rub the chalk on its side over the entire surface of the chalkboard. Once the board is completely covered in chalk, use a chalkboard eraser or a dry cloth and completely rub it all off. You will now have a board that has a slightly duller gray look to it, but it will be a lot easier for you to use.

When your board is well seasoned, get all your tools ready and find yourself a flat surface in good light where you can work. Get comfortable and keep some paper handy, so you can sketch out any designs wher inspiration hits. Planning your artwork out first rather than sketching directly onto the board makes the process less daunting. As you already know, lettering can be divided into three main groups. Let's see how these are affected by lettering with chalk.

Script

Script chalk lettering is the perfect style to use for chalkboards that you want to look "pretty" for fancy events like parties. Modern calligraphy-style lettering looks great on chalkboards because it's the perfect mi modern and vintage and is a really easy look to achie

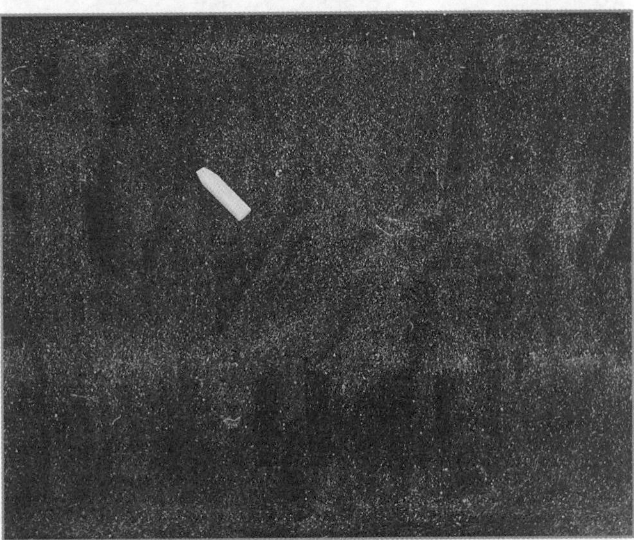

Sans Serif

This is really easy to create on a chalkboard, as it's just normal writing but using chalk! Sans serif can be used for chalk lettering to give a more modern feel. It also looks great when incorporated into a design that uses multiple styles of lettering.

Serif

This is another great look for chalkboards, and is easy to do, as you just add "feet" to your lettering. Serif lettering has a more vintage look (think of old newspapers), but can look really elegant when paired with script lettering on a chalkboard.

Within these three basic groups there is a lot of room for customization and variety. The best thing about chalk lettering is that your design will be unique to you because no one else draws letters exactly the same way. So chalk lettering is a great skill to show off your own unique flair! A handy hint for whatever style you choose is that once you've laid out your guidelines you should work from the top to the bottom of your board. Nothing is more maddening than having crafted a beautiful word at the bottom of your board only for you to accidentally smudge it when you move back up to the top! Generally, it's also a good idea to also work from the left-hand to the right-hand side of the board to make sure you leave enough space for each word. If you're left-handed it can also be a good idea to use your right hand as a wrist-rest beneath the line of lettering you're working on to avoid smudging.

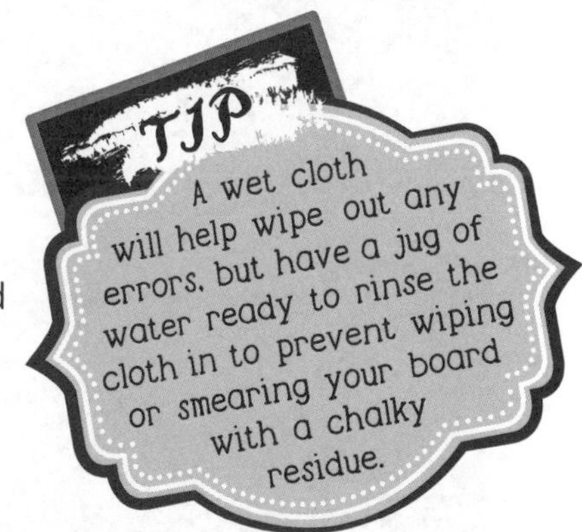

Drawing YOUR LAYOUT

It's always a good idea to sketch some initial small-scale designs with pencil and paper before starting. This will give you a basic idea of what you want the board to look like before you start chalking.

Let's practice together. Pick a quote you'd like to letter (shorter is generally better when you're first learning) and draw about three to five little sketches on paper first. Pick the most important words in the phrase and emphasize them.

Consider the different lettering styles you want to use (three maximum so it's not too busy!) as well as the tone of the piece; for example, elegant script styles work well for event boards, whereas a spooky-looking lettering style would be best for a Halloween board.

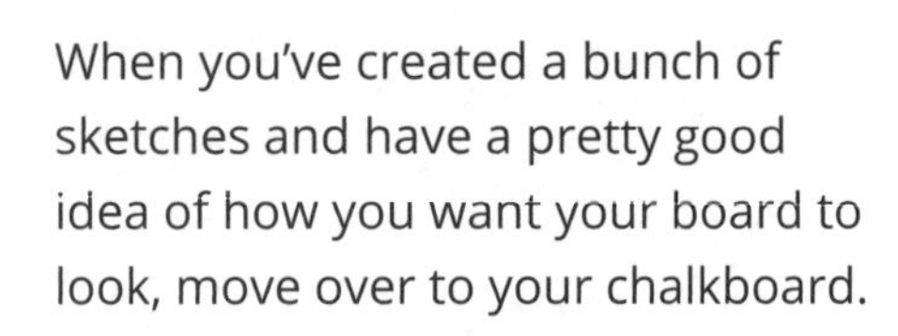

When you've created a bunch of sketches and have a pretty good idea of how you want your board to look, move over to your chalkboard.

You'll need to sketch the basic layout on your board to make sure everything fits, is centered, and has the right proportions. Always sketch lightly, especially when drawing guidelines on your board and when drawing the basic outline of your letters. Chalk is easy to erase if you make a mistake, but it's a lot easier to build up the strength of the chalk line by going over it a few times than to struggle to erase any mistakes made in a strong chalk outline.

Once your guides are on the board, you can start filling in and adding weight to the rest of your letters and decorations. Because chalk is thicker than pencil, you'll need to leave plenty of space between the individual letters, especially if you're drawing letters with serifs and decorative elements like shadows. You'll most likely be erasing elements quite often; remember you can always clean up with a cotton bud, especially if this is your first board. Don't give up—awesome final chalk masterpieces will be well worth the wait!

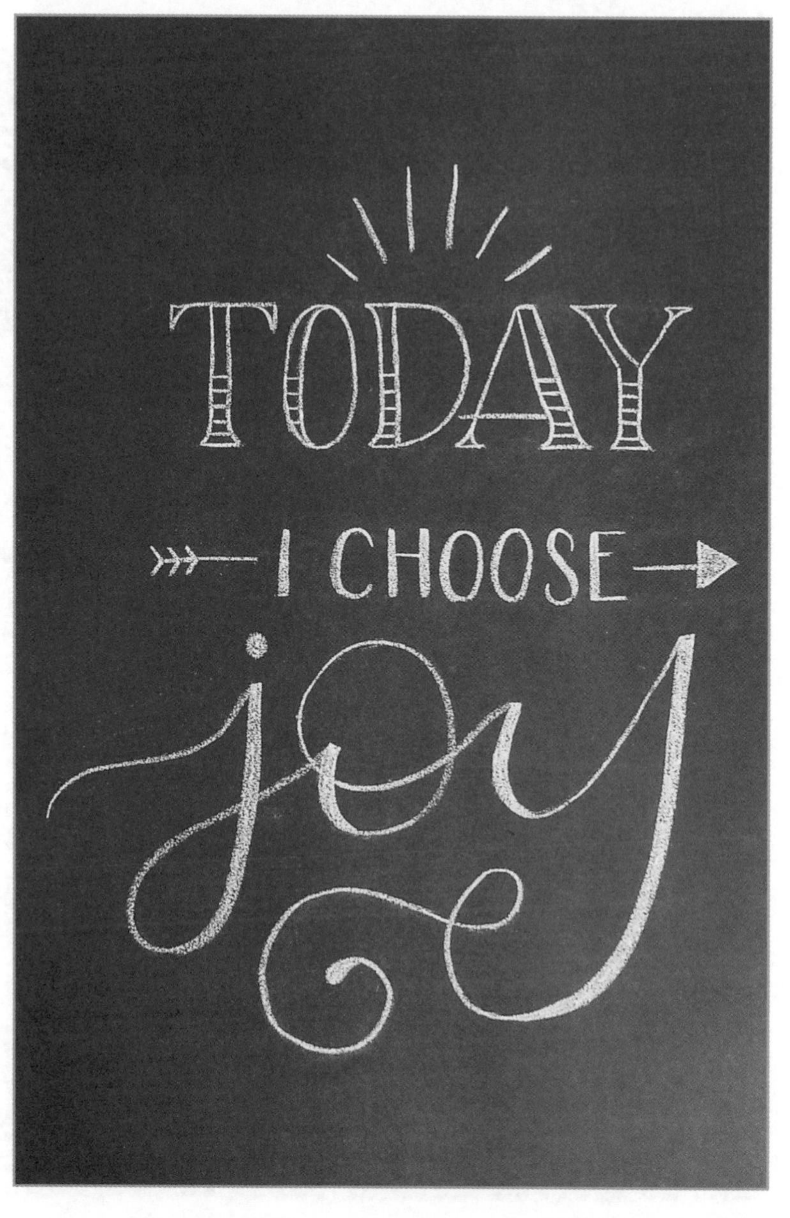

When you add effects and decorations to your chalk lettering (like shadows, in-line text decorations, flourishes swirls, floral elements, and borders), it's important to remember your chalk will draw a thicker line than a pencil. You'll need to allow extra space for this when you draw your design, otherwise it will look too cramped.

Like all hand-lettering, to make sure that your shadows look right and are consistent, you need to make sure the light source is coming from the same location. For all these examples in "Embellishments" below, the light source is coming from the right of the letter (see the sun next to letter A), so the shadow will always be on the left side. There are lots of different ways to draw shadows with chalk, from a simple line shadow (A and D), to a solid shadow (C), to a lined shadow (B), or you could even try combining these styles!

In contrast, in-line text decorations are embellishments that you add to the inside of your letters to give them more personality. Examples D and E show two different kinds, but you can experiment and create plenty more of your own, provided you've left room for them in your letters. When decorating, don't forget to keep the tip of your chalk sharpened to make sure you can draw those finer lines accurately!

Embellishments

Other around-letter flourishes can really work well to decorate and accentuate your chalk lettering, like floral corner decorations, arrows, full frames, and banners. The examples on this spread should give you a good sense of some simple but effective decorations to practice.

Florals

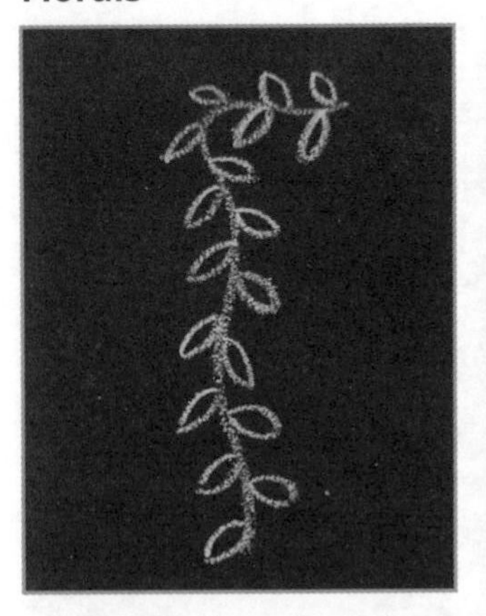

Arrows

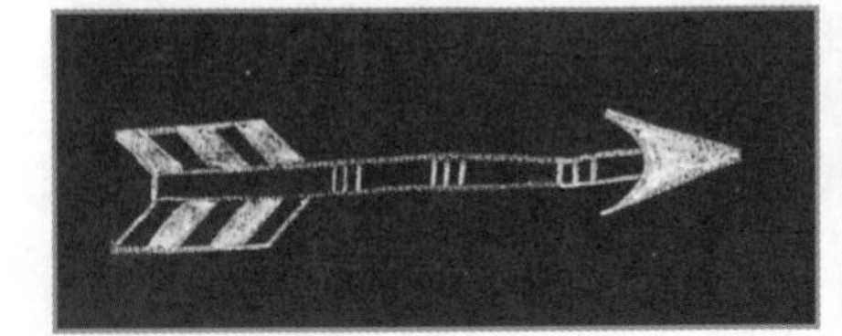

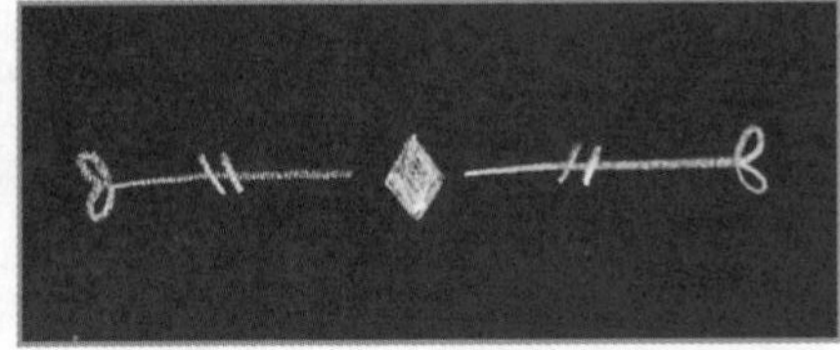

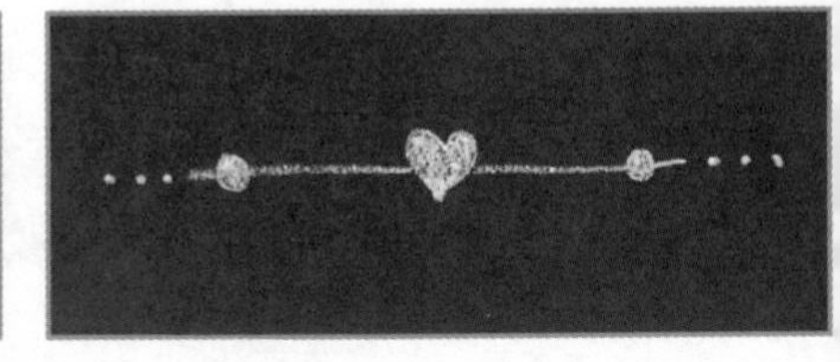

Frames

Banners

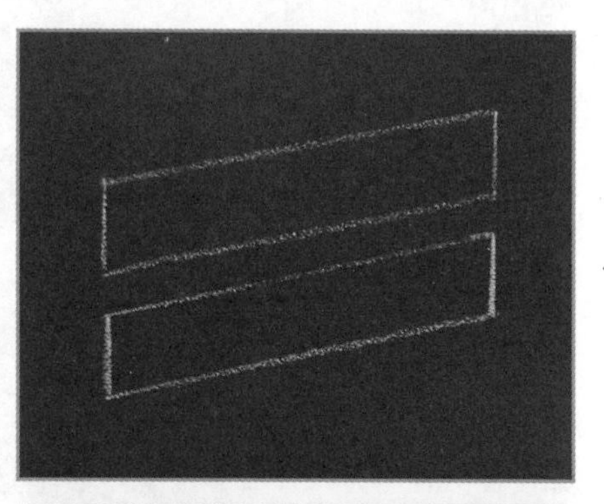

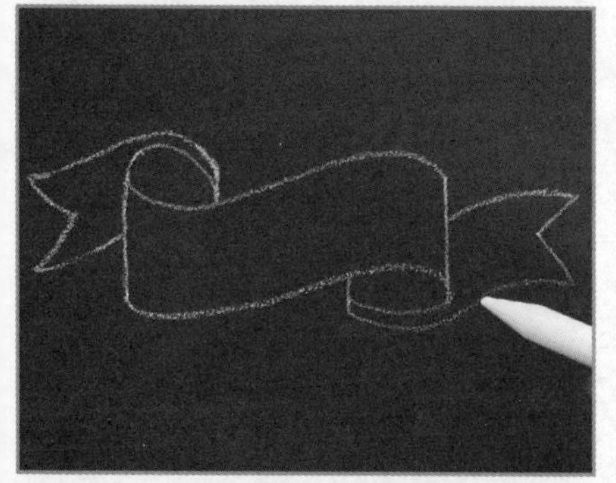

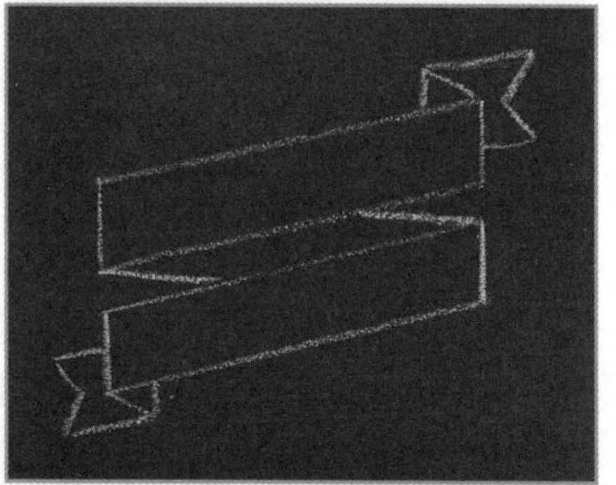

Transfer Technique

The great thing about hand-lettering is that you're usually creating a one-off and unique design every time: however, as an alternative option, you can also create your own chalk-lettering templates which you can then transfer onto chalkboards. This technique is useful if you're not confident about being able to draw the piece directly onto the board and want to ease into doing chalk-lettering free-form. It's also useful if you want to incorporate computer-generated fonts of images into your chalk-lettering.

1. Either draw your design on a piece of paper or create it using a word processing or design program on your computer and print it out. Before sticking any of the paper to the board, coat the back of your paper with the side of a piece of chalk: then you can stick it to the board in the position you want. If your board is bigger than the paper, you can cut out each word separately before sticking it to your board with either adhesive putty or sticky tape (this is particularly handy if you're working on a huge board or wall). However, if your paper fits nicely onto the board, just stick it to the board in one piece.

2. Using a pencil, trace over the design on the paper. By doing this, you are transferring the chalk you've just rubbed from the back of the paper onto the board, leaving a faint design in chalk on the board.

3. Once you've traced over the entire design, remove your paper guides. You should be left with a faint chalk outline. Now you can retrace over the design with either chalk or chalk pens to complete it. Chalk pens are usually used to "set" the design in this technique as they are more vibrant and their results last a lot longer. If you're using chalk but want it to be more vibrant and last longer, dip the tip of the chalk in a drop of water before drawing. This technique takes some getting used to—if you use too much water, you'll end up with soggy chalk!

4. You may well need to clean up a few areas of the design. This can be done with a wet cloth or a cotton tip dipped in water.

TIP

If you're using chalk pens, be mindful that the pens will pick up some of the chalk dust as you are tracing over it. You'll need to give your pens a break every now and then to make sure they don't get too clogged up and stop working properly.

This is going to be a merry message—something for a special holiday, a party perhaps, or greetings to friends for a sleepover.

1. Grab your board and your sharpened chalk, and (very) lightly draw some guidelines. For this project, we will draw a circle as well as straight lines to mark the center, both vertically and horizontally.

2. Start by drawing the base guidelines of your letters. Remember to be super light with your touch at this point, as you want to be able to easily erase any mistakes. Don't forget about the size and proportion of the words to each other, as well as the spacing between letters and words. Place the middle of each word on the central vertical line and then work outwards from there. "EAT," "drink," and "BE MERRY" are the only words here, so letter them large in sans-serif style to completely fill the circle and to attract the most attention. Because "drink" is about liquid, make the lettering look fluid.

3. Once you are happy with the design—where it is placed, how it looks, etc.,—start to fill out the body of your letters. It's still useful to draw lightly though, as it is always easier to keep building up chalk strength than trying to remove a mistake.

4. When you are happy with the letters, you can add decorations. For this seasonal board, I have included a wreath, holly, and stars. Adding the decorations last allows you to make the most of the space for lettering without getting distracted by the decorations. Don't forget to keep your hand off the letters you have already drawn—you don't want to smudge them! You can now proudly display your chalkboard art for all to enjoy during the festive season.

Sweet 16 Pool Party

Now it's time to take your art to the streets! (Well, outside anyway.) Get permission first (very important), then grab your chalks and head over to the walls and sidewalks—your canvases. Show off your art to the great wide world!

1. Since you'll be working outside for this project, you'll need to prep the area a little. If working on a brick wall, you'll need to brush it down with a broom to make sure you've gotten rid of any dirt or (gasp) cobwebs!

2. Lightly sketch your guides on the wall with chalk. Use sharpened chalk as it makes a lighter mark. Or, if you've already drawn a full-size sketch for this project, you can use the transfer technique to get it centered and in the right place. If you're working freehand, sketch some light guides and use a wet cloth to erase any mistakes.

3. After you're happy with the light guidelines you've drawn, you can fill in the letters. You'll need to keep sharpening the chalk to make sure you get a sharp point to work with. Don't be distracted by the different surfaces of walls and paths: you still need to work from top to bottom and left to right. The surface is unlikely to be even, but it doesn't matter. Carry on anyway: it will be part of the character of the piece.

4. Once you're happy with the letters and overall shape, use a wet cloth to clean up any mistakes you've made along the way. Because the surface that you're working on is not smooth, you will need to use a much wetter cloth to do this. However, be careful it's not so soaked it drips down and ruins your design, unless that's what you want to go for, really emphasizing the idea of a pool party! After you've tidied it up a little you can add any extra decorations you want. You now have a gorgeous piece of outside lettering. This is a really cool idea for a pool party or barbecue.

TIP

You will go through a LOT of chalk for this outside project, as you're working on a rougher surface than usual. Make sure you have plenty of chalk handy. I went through at least four pieces!

Caitlin's
SWEET 16
POOL PARTY

The Adventure *begins*

Special events are the perfect opportunity for a spectacular chalkboard. They also make an awesome present if you create them for someone else to add to their special day. Place it somewhere prominent to announce the occasion—a beach party, garden fete, barbecue, or sports day. This example is for a family wedding. It can be the first thing that the guests see and it's also the perfect wedding present!

1. On your freshly seasoned board, grab a sharpened chalk and lightly draw your guidelines. For this design we will draw a prominent central banner and some other straight guidelines for the rest of the lettering. But also allow room for a simple but cute border around the names of the couple getting married. Make sure you work lightly so you can easily erase if you need to. As with all chalkboard projects, you will need to sharpen your chalk between every few strokes to keep a super-crisp line.

2. Begin by lightly drawing the basic guidelines for your letters; think about spacing, size, and proportion. For an unusual twist, make the usually unimportant word "and" really prominent, right at the top of the chalkboard. It gives a sense of their romantic journey continuing but also marking a new beginning. I have also drawn in the guidelines for my banner, so that I can make sure the word underneath it doesn't come too close.

3. This design uses three different lettering styles: serif, sans serif, and a ribbon style of script. When the light guidelines are in place, and if you are happy with the placement of your letters, you can start to fill them in and add weight and depth. Try not to smudge your work as you go!

4. Now that you have the letters in place, you can clean up any mistakes you may have made. Use a cotton tip for this because it is a lot easier to get into the finer details! You now have a gorgeous board that you can show off with pride.

Weekly Planner

Making a lettering design for an interactive chalkboard is really cool, as it can be added to, erased, and then reused, over and over again. For this project, we're going to create an interactive chalkboard to make a weekly planner for you and your family to get everyone organized!

1. First, grab a seasoned chalkboard and start drawing some light guidelines. This board has been measured and divided into eight sections—the heading, plus the days of the week. The top section is a little bigger to leave room for the heading. Sketch the heading in and then put the letters for each day of the week in seven equal sections down the left-hand side, making sure to leave plenty of room for the reminders and notes you can add later.

2. Once you've lightly sketched your guides on the board with chalk, grab a chalk pen and start drawing over the top of your guides. You should rule your lines originally with chalk, but then use a chalk pen to go over them freehand to achieve a less straight and so less formal look. You should then have a board that is almost complete! If you haven't already, fill in the letters to give them weight and add any decorative elements you like.

3. Wait for the chalk pens to dry (preferably overnight to be extra sure), and then erase the entire board with a dry (but soft) cloth or a chalk duster. It's important your cloth is clean and soft as you will be applying a gentle yet firm pressure—anything even slightly scratchy in texture might scrape off your chalk pen work. You will now have a gorgeous and unique weekly planner for your home, which not only looks great but will help keep your busy schedules in order!

TIP

It's super helpful to have a piece of paper near you to test your chalk pen each time before you draw on the board. Sometimes there is dust or old chalk stuck on the pen, or occasionally it can leak out a little too quickly. Having the testing paper really helps to avoid such unnecessary problems.

Weekly
PLANNER
M Basketball practice
T
W Soccer training
Th
F Dinner at Dad's
Sa Swimming
Su Brunch - 10:30

Monday
tuesday
Wednesday
thursday
Friday
Saturday
Sunday

Welcome TO OUR HOME

For this project we're going to create a gorgeous chalkboard to put at the entrance of your home. This also makes a perfect gift, such as a Mothers' Day gift. Alternatively, you can change this to welcome people to your room in style!

1. Firstly, grab a seasoned chalkboard and draw some super-light guidelines. To design the message on a slant, draw diagonal parallel lines, with the lower pair extra wide for "HOME." Once you've got your guidelines in place, you can (again—very lightly) draw in the basic outlines of your letters.

2. This time our project is short, sweet, and to the point, so it is most effective presented unfussily. While there are three different types of lettering, there are only a couple of restrained flourishes. In this instance "HOME" is the most important word, so it has been outlined to be much bigger than the other words and with plenty of width so that you can add some in-letter decoration.

3. After filling in your letters, you can add in-line decorations (for this one I've added dots inside the word "HOME"), shadows, and any other decorative flourishes and illustrations you like. I've drawn a cute house, but you could add anything from flowers or a sketch of your family to a silhouette of your pet or favorite animal. You now have a beautiful board to welcome visitors!

For this project we're creating an enticing chalkboard menu for a special meal with loved ones. It's good enough to eat!

TIP It's super handy to have a copy of your menu written out on paper first (you don't want to forget anything!). Keep it close to you as you draw on your board— it makes the entire process less daunting when you can plan out the words.

1. Grab a chalkboard (seasoned or unseasoned—your choice) and draw a few really light guidelines. I've kept mine to a minimum as I really want this board to look handmade and not too perfect, but it's up to you. After you've sketched your light guidelines, you can draw in the heading (I've gone with a simple "Menu" but you could always make things interesting with "Let's eat!" or similar), and lightly sketch in your menu items. You can use lettering to differentiate between different elements of the menu. For instance, the lettering has been split so that it's easy to distinguish between the starter and main course. The principal ingredient is in capitals and the accompanying sides are in italic script. You'll likely have to erase and redraw a few times to make sure you get things looking right.

2. Once you've drawn in your menu, erase your guidelines with a cotton tip or chalk duster. If you're happy with the overall design, you can now begin giving your letters some weight. I've made "Menu" and "enjoy" thicker so that they stand out.

3. Now you should have a tasty looking menu! To make it even better, you can add any decorative or illustrative bits you like; I've gone with a simple leaf illustration at the top and a complementary leaf border at the bottom. You now have a super menu chalkboard to impress and tempt everyone!

Chalkboard messages can be as simple or sophisticated as you like. They can be a deep philosophical thought, a line from your favorite song, or a motivational saying. The fun is in the planning and drawing of the lettering, and the satisfaction from a piece of work made with love.

DESIGN
&
CREATE!
MyE.
De Leon.

DESIGN & CREATE!

Hand-lettering is used on all types of artwork, crafts, and even for commercial products: think book covers, cards, T-shirts, mugs, posters, billboards, and more! There are loads of ways to use lettering every day: put fancy lettering on your schoolbooks, use it on hand-written notes to your friends, create special creations like posters, and even make a chore list suddenly look enticing! This section explores a range of really fun projects that you can create with your newfound lettering skills.

In this chapter, you will learn the importance of design and composition in creating your lettering artworks. While lettering gives you more freedom of artistic expression than typing or normal writing, you still need to follow a few simple rules if you want to create artwork that will really stand out. Like typography (the art and technique of arranging type, discussed in the first section), the spacing above, around, and between letters and words is very important for balancing your lettering artwork.

Where to start

To make stunning pieces of lettering artwork, you need to understand how the lettering and art styles work together. What makes a composition gel? How can you make your art stand out from the rest? The real secret behind great lettering is to love what you do and just have fun with it! Like any skill, the more you do it, the better you'll get. Play with the letters, experiment, and explore! And you never know, maybe one day lettering could be your career!

Find things to draw inspiration from—maybe use a leaf instead of a brush pen to write letters, or create your own textures using scrap items. Try working with different inks and paints and discover what a difference a change of color can make to even a simple design.

Also keep your eyes open when you are out and about; lettering and typography are everywhere. Lettering that catches your eye is lettering that works! This section is packed with amazing tricks, tips, projects, and inspiration to get you started—so let's go!

Composition TRICKS & TIPS

If you want to create a piece that looks good and works just the way you want it to, it is crucial that you combine different lettering styles together effectively. Think about what you are trying to do. Don't make your letters too random; create a great composition by planning how you'll balance the piece with a combination of different styles. Think through all the different ways you could make it work, and choose the best parts carefully. The key is to experiment a lot—it's all part of the fun! Let's look at some of the thought that went into the following lettering artworks.

Play around with the composition and letter styles as much as you can. Here, the bold statement is also reflected in the artwork's bold style and long radiating lines! Also notice that the short words occupy the smaller spaces between the big words. As for the big words, they are styled to stand out, particularly the emphasized words of "anyone" and "sparkle."

This letter artwork was designed to fit an A4 or letter piece of paper that can hang above a desk or workspace, to provide inspiration all day long. The composition was very carefully planned using a ruler to create guidelines to make sure the letters work in proportion to each other.

After completing the text layout it was clear that something was missing around the empty corners. In cases like this it can work well to play around with different patterns to fill this empty space. Here, an art deco style nicely echoes the grand inspirational phrase.

Experimenting with different patterns can also help you discover new things. Check out historic art styles such as art deco and art nouveau for ways to add embellishments to your lettering!

The lettering in this layout is more informal and so the style and message work well with a softer and more fluid decoration than on the artwork above. Instead of a formal border, some floral flourishes around the letters make for a beautiful composition. As a final touch, you can see how adding little dots around the wreath makes this artwork look soft and whimsical.

Inspirational POSTERS

Inspirational posters are a great way to create lettering works of art and practice rules of compositions. The below quote fits using Blackletter hand-lettering. The word "WISDOM" suggests something strong and timeless, which is characteristic of the Blackletter style. Because this style looks very dominant in the composition, the rest of the letters should be created in a plainer style. For the finishing touches, a few curls and spirals nicely fill the empty spaces.

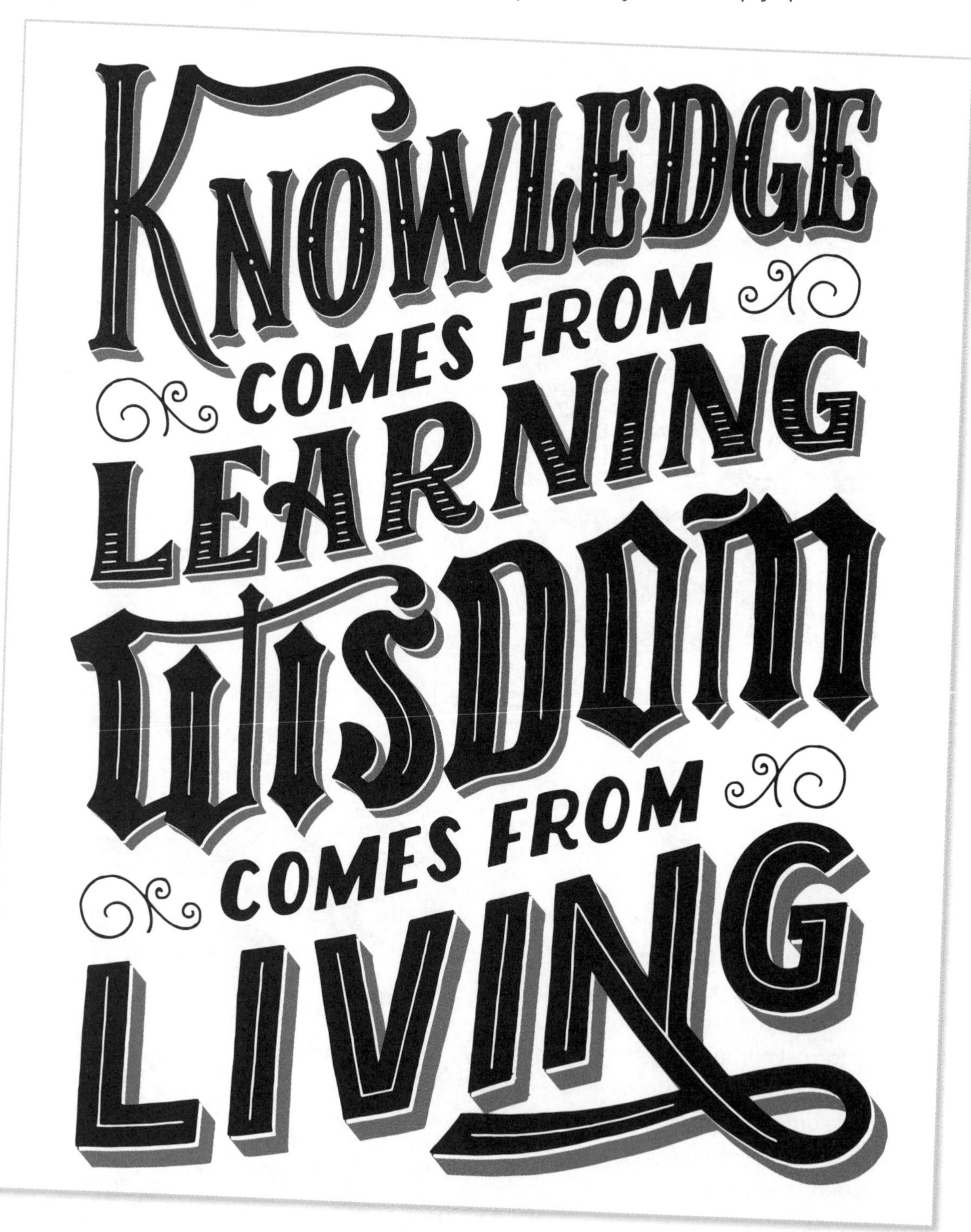

Find a phrase you like and have a go at making a motivational poster. Try to convey the mood of the words through your lettering and use some of these tips and tricks to make it fill the page neatly.

Let's look at a few ways to amend a lettering design work if it's not initially going quite the way you planned!

Here is a neat trick for turning what was a horizontal (called landscape) composition into an upright vertical (called portrait) one. This piece started out as a landscape layout, but as it progressed, it was clear that the design called for a portrait shape. Instead of redoing the lettering, adding extended flourishes to the top and bottom of the layout elongated it to fit the new shape!

The arch lettering at the bottom of "WAKE UP" created an empty space in the middle. Placing the shorter, non-emphasized words inside a semi-banner format filled the empty space and complemented the overall composition. Job done!

This artwork was created without any formal planning or spacing to fit a square composition—no measurements, no rulers, and no guides! As a result it is a fun design that is very loose and creative.

This is a good example of how mistakes can actually become opportunities. Due to a miscalculation of letter width, after drawing the "AL" of "ALMOST" there wasn't enough room left to finish the word. However, by making the "OST" smaller the result was still punchy and playful! After lettering all the words, it looked a bit retro, so it suited a decorative retro style— e.g. filling all the spaces with filigrees and teardrop shapes. Adding extra patterns under "OST" also made this smaller lettering seem intentional and look great.

Patterned LETTERS

Decorate your letters! Try drawing your letter outlines and then filling them with different patterns. Not only is this a unique approach to drawing letters, but it will inspire lots of original combinations in your artwork too!

Start with easy patterns—lines, dots, curves, swirls—then try some repeating shapes like squares, circles, and triangles. Experiment with what happens when you flip them in other directions. The key is to enjoy the process and don't stress too much. Check out the word "CUTE" and the examples of patterns below, then try decorating the letters yourself. Drawing repeating patterns can be therapeutic and super fun!

Play with your patterns! Design your own creations in the boxes and then use them to fill in the "FUN" outlines. Stick with black and white for a striking monochrome effect or go mad with color; but above all, have FUN!

MONOGRAMS

Monograms consist of two or more letters, which are often a person's initials. The letters are overlapped to create one symbol. Monograms are often used as logos, in jewelry, and on high-end accessories. What's fun about drawing monograms is working out how you will interlock the layers of each letter to create a beautiful piece of art. Start with your own initials, or try those of your family or best friends, and then use the monogram on letters and birthday cards. You could even scan your monogram and use it as your personal logo for emails and online messaging! Here are some ideas to get you started.

The initials "STU" are a bit tricky, but are great fun to interlock. Give this monogram a more vintage feel by using ornate serif lettering.

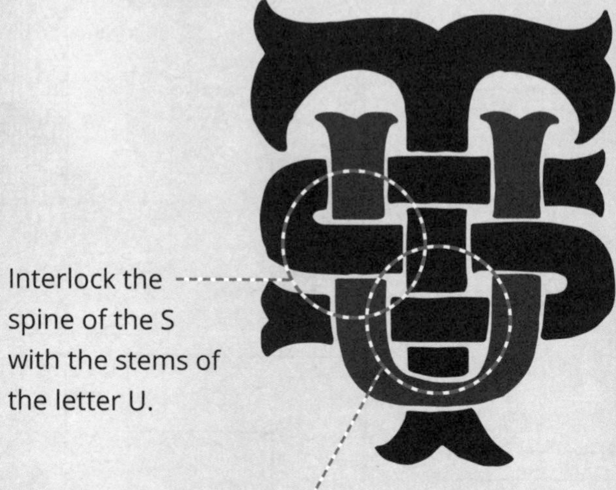

Interlock the spine of the S with the stems of the letter U.

The letter T has a vertical stem that can occupy the white space created by the U, and is the perfect stroke to create an alternating lock with the S.

Using a sans-serif style here makes things easier and also creates a more contemporary feel. These initials are quite challenging, but there's always a way to work with letters, so don't give up!

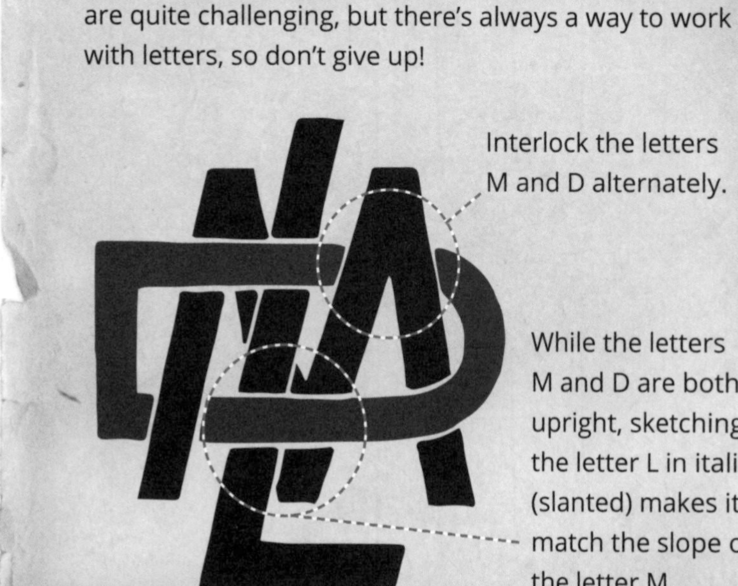

Interlock the letters M and D alternately.

While the letters M and D are both upright, sketching the letter L in italics (slanted) makes it match the slope of the letter M.

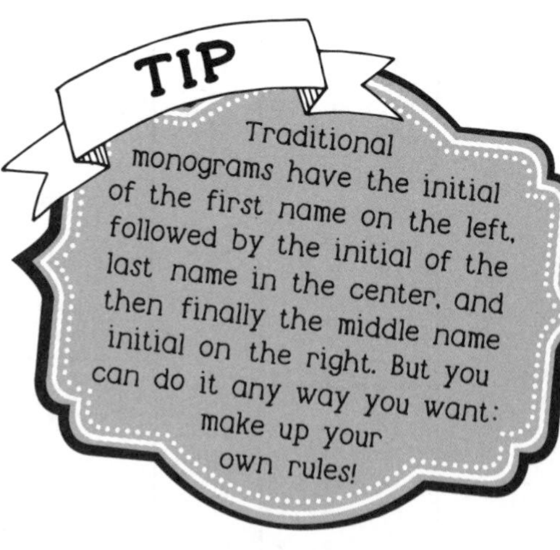

This script style combines the letters "SRS." Having the same letter on either side adds symmetry, but also gives scope to play with little differences as well, such as treating their terminals (the end parts of the letter) differently.

Extend the letter S so that it becomes the beginning flourish of the R.

Interlock the stem of letter R to the spine of the S.

Extend the leg of the letter R to turn into the terminal of the S.

Using a loopy script style to entangle the monogram letters can look super cool! The combination of the letters "NBL" has many possibilities, such as twining the strokes around each other like rope.

Connect the final stroke of the letter N to the entry stroke of the B.

Create a loop by hooking the opening stroke of the L to the top bowl of the B.

Interlock the lower bowl of the B to the L.

"VCW" is an interesting combination for trying out the style of horizontal looping, because the V and W have similarities, while the letter C is quite different. However, the C has an open center and is therefore great to fit the W and V into. It looks a bit like a paperclip in this design!

Position the V along the apex of the W and intertwine the letters.

Lock the strokes together by creating a loop.

A two-letter monogram is quite common. This one uses the initials "AK." If you let your letters share the same letter stem, it adds to the sense of the letters being united, and is very effective.

Decorate your terminals! They don't have to be boring.

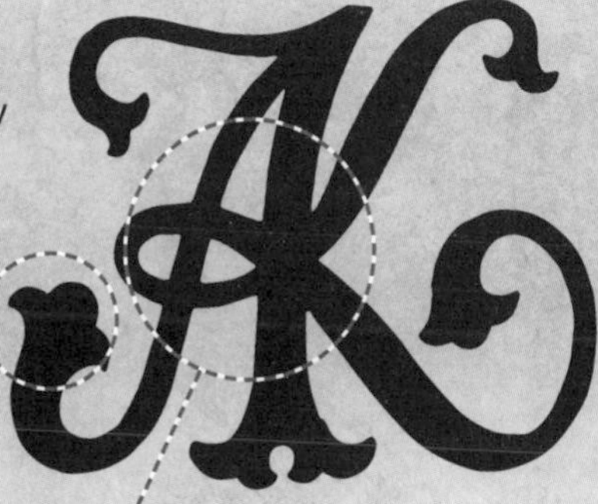

The letter A and the letter K share a stroke.

Numbers & SYMBOLS

"Lettering" doesn't mean that you only draw the characters of the alphabet! Numbers and symbols are great fun to learn as well, and are just as beautiful as the twenty-six letters of the alphabet!

Here are some examples to inspire you. Start copying some of the numbers on this page, and then apply these styles to other numbers and symbols. It's also fun to experiment with different tools to letter them with. The possibilities are endless!

”@1$%59
2?6!$4#
#

Birthday CARDS & ENVELOPES

Personalized hand-lettered greeting cards are a sure way to show someone just how much you love them. You'll also have fun making them! Try composing your cards using different styles—formal, cute, or just plain quirky. Then try adding some decorations or illustrations to make it even more interesting.

Who says birthday envelopes have to be boring? Make them fun and pretty by using lettering to personalize the name and address of the recipient. You could create a nice touch by adding a little styling to suit him or her, like creating leaf and flower flourishes for someone who loves the outdoors or adding a puppy and a paw border for a dog lover! Then match it with your personalized greeting card!

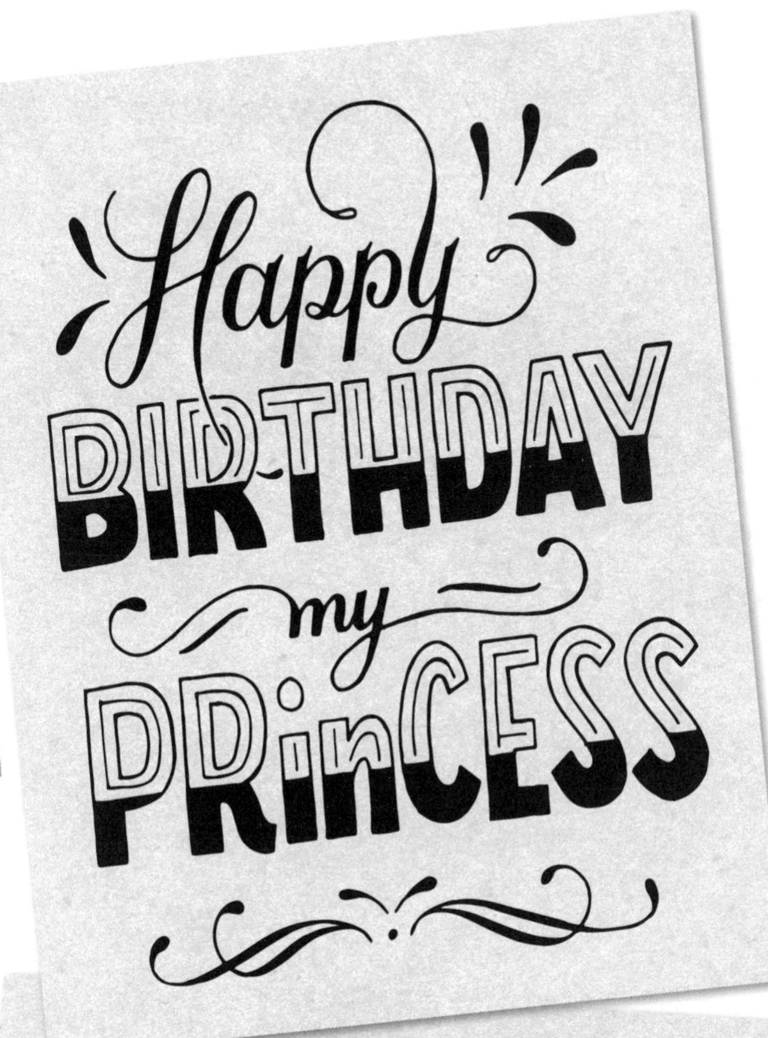

TIP

Don't leave too much empty space on your envelopes and cards! You can add simple curly flourishes to fill them up and add more interest to your work: just don't overdo it.

Leila
GIBSON
123 WALNUT DR.
ARIZONA, 56789 USA

Birthday CARDS & ENVELOPES

Make an envelope more exciting by playing with your letter shapes: vary the sizes, fill them in, or perhaps add a little decoration. Just make sure that all the post-office workers can easily read your envelope, so it gets to the right address! You also need to make sure that you leave room for the postage stamps!

UNIT D TANCINCO SUBD.
TAYTAY, RIZAL 1900
PHILIPPINES

Now it's your turn!

Draw a card and matching envelope design. When you're happy with it, transfer it to a separate card and envelope and send it out into the world. Your friends and family will be amazed and delighted when they open their mailbox and find this treasure inside!

Do you love reading books? Making your own meaningful bookmarks means that you'll never lose your page again! Why not try adding an uplifting quote or a phrase from your favorite book, or about the joy of reading itself? Style each bookmark differently and include illustrations for a bit of fun! These can also make great gifts for book lovers. Check out the below design ideas.

TIP

Remember that vertical compositions work best for bookmarks. You don't have to fill the entire shape with artwork—sometimes less is more! Try shorter one- or two-word phrases and add illustrative flourishes to fill up the rest of the space.

Choose a phrase, style it out, and ink it in!
These make great gifts.

Digitizing LETTERING

Once you have got the hang of hand-lettering, you may want to try turning your pieces into digital artwork. This allows you to share your lettering online, make small changes to your design (like duplicating flourishes or adding dashes of color), or save your art for later use in other projects.

To digitize your art you will need access to a computer and a scanner. As this process can be quite complicated and requires some technical skill, you may need someone to assist you, like an experienced adult.

There are many different programs you can use to digitize your lettering, ranging from free software like Inkscape and GIMP, to programs that you need to pay for like Adobe Photoshop and Adobe Illustrator. When you're starting out, you only need the basic features included with most free programs, which makes free software a fantastic resource.

Each program has a different layout and specific tools, but don't be put off: these steps will provide you with the basic process to digitize your lettering. Once you have chosen a program to use, check out its instructions and look up anything you're not sure about through the "help" function within the program.

Digitizing your Lettering

1. Finalize your hand-lettered artwork. It is best to ink it in, as some scanners can't pick up faint pencil lines. Make sure you scan a clean piece of artwork without any smudges or half-erased lines, as it's extremely time-consuming to remove these marks digitally. If you do have a very smudgy piece of artwork, trace it onto a fresh page first.

Pencil sketch with embellishments.

2. Scan in your artwork. If you can, set your scanner to a minimum of "300 dpi." This refers to the quality of the image. A higher number makes for a crisper image. If your scanner can support it, you can even scan in at 600 dpi!

TIP

When digitizing lettering, if you have letters that overlap within a design, it's better to separate them out before inking and scanning them. Once you have vectorized them digitally, you can them overlap them again. This will allow you to apply different effects to each letter, and to make adjustments to the layout if needed.

Inked sketch, ready to scan at 300 dpi or higher.

Adjusted scan where the white and black areas have been accentuated.

3. Open your scanned-in lettering with your image-editing software, such as Adobe Photoshop or GIMP. Use the "eraser" tool to remove any specks or extra lines that you do not want in your finished piece. You should also adjust the contrast to make the black lines darker and the white areas whiter to help the vectorizing program you're about to used recognize your different letters and shading.

4 a. Next, open your scanned-in image in an illustration software program like Adobe Illustrator or Inkscape. Use a "trace" function to convert your lettering into "vector" shapes. In some programs you can do this automatically, but still also have the option to manually make adjustments. Play with the settings in your chosen program until you are happy with how your artwork looks.

b. Once you have converted your letters to vectors, select the group of shapes and click "expand" and then "ungroup." This will allow you to amend each letter-shape individually.

c. If you're not happy with the result of the automatic trace function, you can instead digitally trace your artwork by hand. Use the "pen" tool in your program to do this. This will create a cleaner finish to the edges of your artwork. If you want to preserve that original hand-drawn quality though, you can then also apply "brush" tool effects along the edges to make them a little rougher.

TIP

"Vectorizing" your artwork means converting it to a format that can be made bigger or smaller without losing its resolution or looking blurry. This means you can resize your artwork to fit a small postcard, or blow it up to hang as a poster on your wall.

SHINE LIKE The WHOLE UNIVERSE

Automatic "traced" version of the lettering, which turned the artwork into vector shapes and then had color adjusted.

5. Once the trace is complete, you can easily move things around, erase sections, and add color! You could even try applying different effects and in different combinations. Save them as different files and compare them at the end to see which you like best! You may find that once you've finished digitizing your hand-lettered artwork, it still needs a little something extra. In which case, you can duplicate flourishes and accents to add more detail. You can also remove or erase sections if you feel the piece is too busy. Look up how to perform these functions in your particular program. If there is just one word or section that you are not happy with, you can always just erase it, re-draw it on paper, scan it in, vectorize it, and then add it into your original piece.

Digitized version with outer white stroke and drop shadow added.

Remember, learning a new skill can take time and practice. Don't worry if it takes a while to learn the software or if your first digital project doesn't turn out quite the way you hoped. Just keep practicing and soon you'll be wowing all your friends with your fantastic digitized hand-lettering!

Combining LETTERING with PHOTOGRAPHY

Now that you know how to digitize your lettering, you can combine it with photos to create eye-catching artwork. There are many apps to help you do this, but if you want to personalize these photos, you can simply digitize your lettering (see instructions on pages 188–189) and then apply it over a digital or scanned photo.

Once you have finished digitizing your lettering, open your photograph in a photo-editing program like Adobe Photoshop or GIMP. You need to do what's called "adding a new layer." There will be a simple menu or tool option to do this. Your photo will be on one layer (let's call it layer 1) and your lettering needs to be on another layer (layer 2). When you select layer 1, you only edit or move the photo, while when you select layer 2, you only move or edit the hand-lettering. When both are selected you can see what your final picture will look like. You can select the lettering layer and adjust the opacity (how see-through something is) and the color or tone of the hand-lettering as needed to work with your photo.

This is another way to personalize meaningful memories to turn into keepsakes for yourself, your friends, or your family.

Perspective

KEEP on SHINING

Project INSPIRATION

Congratulations! You've made it through an amazing range of lettering styles, techniques, mediums, and projects. Your mind must be bursting with ideas and your hand itching to do some more lettering! You have all that you need to go make your own hand-lettered mark on the world!